Leadership Tales of a Corporate Nobody

A Corporate America Navigation Guide

By: Daniel Vaccaro

TABLE OF CONTENTS

Dedication

Acknowledgements

Introduction

Chapter One – The Early Riser

Chapter Two – The Tin Horn

Chapter Three – The Paper Bag

Chapter Four – The Right Decision

Chapter Five – Standing on Your Head

Chapter Six – Eye to Eye

Chapter Seven – Pocket of Excellence

Chapter Eight – Self Fulfilled Prophecy

Chapter Nine – Two Coats of Paint

Chapter Ten – The Window

Chapter Eleven – The Tomato

Chapter Twelve - The Hallway

Chapter Thirteen – The Good Life

A Note From The Author

<u>Acknowledgments</u>

I would like to specifically thank my Grandpa John for all of the wisdom and guidance I had no idea he was bestowing on me until long after he had passed. His quick one-liners and mnemonics that he shared with me served him well as the President of the Bethlehem Steelworkers Union in the 1960s. They now serve as the titles of the chapters in this book. I would also like to give special thanks to my father. He is without a doubt the biggest role model of my life. But not the way you would think. I spent the early portion of my life looking at my father as a cautionary tale and a career path to avoid at all costs. I had always viewed him as a role model of the "don't be that guy" variety. Seeing him come home miserable every day from work wasn't great and I couldn't imagine how someone would continuously put themselves in such an environment. I vowed as a child I would never work in a job that I hated. Little did I know how hard that vow would be to keep. I was fortunate enough to find a line of work that I found fulfilling and challenging. I loved what I did, but it came with a catch. What I found in my own career as I progressed through the corporate America world, was that as much as I loved my job, I hated the environment I had to do it in. As I grew older and I began to experience all of the pitfalls corporate America had to offer for myself, my perception of him changed drastically. After working for large fortune 500 companies, small mom and pop shops, and large private companies, I witnessed firsthand what my father experienced with the trials and tribulations that corporate bureaucracies can provide. It was rather ironic that during the darkest times of my career dealing with inept managers and breathtakingly flawed policies my father served as a great resource to provide suggestions on how to survive through it all. In my attempts to avoid following in his footsteps, I was running away from solutions at the same time.

I am forever grateful for his endurance to wade through the chaos to provide for his family day after day. I still have the cautionary tale perception of him regarding professional fulfillment. However, I could not have asked for a better father and can only hope to live up to the standard he has set as a genuinely caring human being.

I would like to thank Simon Sinek, Jocko Willink, Leif Babin, and Captain D. Michael Abrashoff for inspiring me to write this book. Their work and individual contributions to my leadership style have forever changed my life for the better.

Last but certainly not least I would like to thank my

wife, Heather, for standing by my side through all the heartbreak, 80-hour work weeks, and time away from home. Out of all the people who paid a price for any kind of success I had in my career, hers was the highest. I always tried to make it a point to leave work at work, and home at home, but I wasn't always successful. In fact, I was rarely successful early in my career. In the corporate America world, work follows you home. It interrupts holidays, anniversaries, also follows you on vacation, and everywhere else in between. One of the hardest lessons I ever learned was that no matter how important you think your career and your job is, your family means more. Your family more often than not will always be there for you when corporations and coworkers have long moved on. Even if you don't deserve it. My wife had the patience of a saint. She was on the perpetual back burner and was always playing second fiddle to the company line. I thank God every day that I learned that lesson about family meaning more. I don't demonstrate that behavior anymore, largely due to the people named in this acknowledgment. I just wish for my wife's sake that I wasn't such a slow learner.

__Introduction__

Thank you for taking the time to read this book. I wanted to let you know a little about me so you can have some insight as to where I am coming from. The names of the companies and people mentioned in this book have been changed to protect the privacy of those involved and also for legal and non-disclosure purposes. All of the experiences and interactions described within however, actually occurred. Much to my chagrin, but to your benefit.

Anyone who has worked for an organization in corporate America will attest that in the grand purview of things you are essentially just a number. A nobody. When I was first hired by a Fortune 500 company, I walked in thinking I was Daniel at GloboCorp when, in reality, I was just employee #51556. I had no idea at the time that If I screwed up, employee #51557 would just be there to replace me tomorrow. As I look back at it now, that's just how it is. You're just a number. At least that was my observation. Most high-spirited people who enter corporate America don't realize that, at least not right away. They have an unrealistic expectation on how they will be treated by their new organization.

But it doesn't need to be that way.

There are ways to navigate corporate America where you can make a genuine impact and leave your mark in a positive way. You just need to have the courage to take the necessary action. I never had a guide to help me through the minefield of trial and tribulations that corporate America presents you with while working there. My hope is that my observations and tactics used, that helped me

successfully navigate
through corporate America
will help you in your
journey through your
organization. Whether you
are just looking for the next
promotion, or if you aspire
for leadership in the
company. The information
in this book has something
for all.

I have had the privilege to
work for large Fortune 500
companies. For the
purposes of this book,
those experiences will be
consolidated into one
organization I will refer to
as GloboCorp. I have also
been able to work for small
family corporations, and
mid-sized private
companies. Having worked
in the commercial service
industry on building
systems, I was uniquely
positioned to see the inner
workings and behind the
scenes of most
organizations. Everything
from their customer facing
operation, to their logistics,
to the financial approval
and budgeting processes. I

had worked as an essential vendor in the educational sector, the public and military sector, retail, construction, healthcare, and in the industrial sector. This combined with my time spent in the United States Army has granted me the unique position of having perspective.

Being able to see all walks of life operate in a wide variety of corporate environments can open your eyes to trends and common factors that seem to be the same no matter what the variables. You get to witness trade secrets, best practices, and cautionary tales. Out of all the things I have seen that amazed me, some things stood out way more than others. For example, there is one dirty little secret that no company or organization ever wants to admit. That dirty little secret is that a college degree for any position outside of senior leadership is relatively useless. That's right, I said useless. These organizations all want to focus on their first movers' advantage, their proprietary product, patent, or key value proposition that they believe uniquely differentiates them from their competition. You can't learn any of this in a school, you can only learn it by working for them. This is part of the reason why so many college graduates have a hard time finding work after graduation. They're viewed as a dime a dozen. Even graduates from Ivy league institutions get lumped into this bunch. It's a catch-22. No one will hire you if you don't *have* experience, but no one will hire you to *get* experience.

This is not to disparage the value of a college degree; it's just making friends with reality. In specialized fields like education, engineering, medical and Legal professions these degrees are pre-requisites. However, in reality, the basic fundamentals you learned may serve you some purpose in your role, but all that college degree tells the employer is that you know _how_ to learn. They don't really care about <u>what</u> you learned. Think about it. Have you ever been on a job interview where the hiring manager asked you what your overall GPA was during your sophomore year? No, of course not. All they want to know is if you have that piece of paper. This is because no one can ever be truly prepared to work in a corporate America environment. As soon as you are hired, they are going to tell you to forget everything you know, because they are going to teach you what _they_ want you know, and how "they do things".

Here is where the irony sets in. As vast and as different as corporations can be, when you boil them all down to the root operation, regardless of the industry they serve, they are all the same. This is the reason that movies like *Office Space*, television shows like *The Office*, and comic strips like *Dilbert* are so funny. Their satirical take on the everyday life that people go through while working for one of these organizations is only funny to so many people because of its widespread accuracy. This book will help you understand the environment you are in and help guide you to success in ways that a classroom cannot provide. In full disclosure, you may find that some of the topics covered may not apply to your specific organization, but I would be very surprised if the vast majority of what I describe doesn't make you feel like I am sitting in the cubicle next to you.

Thank you again for taking the time to read this book, and I hope you find it valuable. If you do find it valuable, please share it.

Chapter One

**"If you establish a
reputation as an early riser,
you can sleep till noon."**

Whether you are working in
a large organization or a
small one, one thing is
always a constant, that
constant is human nature.
If you were to take a close
observation of the
workforce in your
organization, and chart it
for productivity, you will
find what is considered to
be a traditional bell curve.
For the purposes of this
book, let's say your
organization has 1000
employees. That chart
would show a small number
of employees at the bottom
left corner gradually
increasing as you move to
the right on the chart up to
250 as productivity
improves, peaking around
500 and then gradually
decreasing as you move

toward the highly productive employees toward the opposite bottom right corner of the chart. This happens for various reasons. Some people are just naturally over-achievers. Some people may have just had enough with the corporate America environment and "checked out", also recently known as "quietly quitting" their job, simply biding their time until a better opportunity falls in their lap, or until they inevitably get downsized or fired. Some are poor performers simply out of spite for past transgressions they had with the organization. They have an axe to grind, and they are going to make the bosses and the company pay for it. True to the bell curve, the vast majority of us are stuck in the middle. While it's not a terrible place to be, you don't want to spend a ton of time here either. The biggest challenge of being stuck in the middle is that you are truly a corporate nobody. You are not tasked with new and challenging assignments. You are often passed over for promotions, and you have that feeling of neglect and hopelessness that leaves you feeling like you are playing football without a scoreboard.

One of my favorite quotes from *The Count of Monte Cristo* by Alexander Dumas is when the Abe Faria is counseling Edmond Dantes in his prison cell. The Abe advises him that the guards only check on prisoners two times a day. Once in the early morning, and once again late in the evening to deliver meals and empty their bedpans. The remaining time they have is up to them to do as they please. The Abe simply tells Edmond **"So, neglect becomes our ally"**. This prison reference is unfortunately the exact same thing that happens in corporate America. More often than not when things go as they should, no one in leadership pays any attention to daily events that transpire. They typically only check in when one of two things happen. Either a deadline is missed, or there was a negative financial impact to the organization. Other than that, they are pretty much blind to all else that moves. So, the question becomes how can you turn that neglect into your ally? It's very simple, but most people don't want to hear the answer.

Volunteer.

I know that word generates a lot of anxiety for many people. However, that anxiety that you are feeling, is you coming out of your comfort zone. That is the only way that you will be able to develop as a professional. I know conventional wisdom would say they can't cut your head off if you don't "stick your neck out". I would simply reply with "No risk, No reward." And that "Fortune favors the bold".

Is there a new pilot program the company is starting? **volunteer.**

Are they are looking for new members to be on a work committee? **Volunteer.**

Do you see a person in a position you want who is overwhelmed? **Volunteer to help them dig out.**

The key to this method is not that you will be great at whatever you volunteer at. It's the fact that you were willing to volunteer and "Stick your neck out" to begin with when no one else would. That shows courage, and initiative. This is especially true when you help out that person in a position or role that you desire.

Many people will look at this and scoff stating, "I'm not getting paid to do their job", or "I don't have time for that" This is a fundamentally flawed way of thinking. Not all payment is monetary. For the people who say that they don't have time, that isn't accurate either.

When someone tells you that they don't have time

for something, they are not stating a *fact,* they are stating a *priority*. When someone says that they "don't have time" for something, what they are actually saying is "This isn't important enough to me." You know this is accurate, because if a task or a goal is important enough to you, you will make time to accomplish it.

By volunteering to assist you are getting "on the job training" for the role you want.

Your assistance to that individual will most likely result in an increase in their productivity and success as well. Should that person get promoted or leave the organization, you already have one foot in the door for the position because you have been doing small elements of it all along. Yes, you are not being financially compensated for that position (yet), but you are getting an investment from the organization in your increased knowledge, and knowledge is powerful.

Not to mention it is much easier and efficient for the company to hire from within than recruiting outside staff that they have to train from scratch.

It is the consistency of this behavior that people tend to notice. Both for the good and for the bad. There will be some that see your behavior as a "kiss-ass", "brown-noser", or "teachers-pet". That is on the negative side of the spectrum, and those comments typically come from those on the underperforming side of the bell curve who are insecure with their position in the organization. They are jealous that they don't have the courage to take the same initiative you do and lash out.

The bottom line is that they are upset because you are making them "look bad". I cannot emphasize this enough. *You must learn to ignore these people.* The only one that is making them look bad is themselves. Your actions to better yourself and improve your career path have no bearing on that person's actions or decisions. The flip side is the positive side of the spectrum. Your immediate supervisors, and those who have influence on your career will see your volunteering and view it as ambition and initiative.

The important part to remember about this side of the spectrum is what I first spoke about in the beginning of this chapter. Human Nature. When you volunteer you must approach it from a position of assistance and authenticity. So, what does that mean? If you were to just walk into someone's office and tell them, "You look like you're overwhelmed, give me part of your workload." You would very quickly be seen as a threat and gunning for someone's job. This would create the exact opposite result you are looking to accomplish. Instead, state your intentions early and often. Leading with statements like "I'm interested in learning more about this role, and If possible, I'd like to volunteer my assistance in helping you if you get overwhelmed." Even if it is a very simple task that gets delegated, it is your first step to being viewed as an asset instead of a threat. Also, the more that you do this behavior, the more you will become depended upon.

This is especially true if the task assigned is undesirable. And make no mistake, when you volunteer, you are going to get the shit jobs and tasks first that no one else wants. That's the reason they are left hanging. It won't be easy, but try to learn to love those tasks. Get comfortable being uncomfortable. This is important because those tasks that no one else wants will provide you with a fast track to gaining experience no one else has. Because you are dealing with the most difficult aspects of the role, all else assigned to you will inevitably become very easy by comparison.

So, in addition to being depended on for your normal role in the company you will bring added value to the table. Now, all of this is dependent on you being able to perform your normal daily task proficiently as well. So, make sure that when you do decide to volunteer you are choosing opportunities that will only serve as a minor inconvenience and not drastically impact your day-to-day role. Some things you will find as you are helping out with these volunteered tasks is that you will learn to think like your superiors in the workplace. Seeing what is important to them and the organization is invaluable. This will also help you be more proficient in your day-to-day role as you will be able to identify what items tasked to you are truly important to the company. It will also help you limit what is essentially just busy work. This allows you to spend the majority of your time making sure that the important tasks are done very well, and the other tasks that no one really cares about anyway are done to an acceptable level, but not taking up any additional time or resources than what is necessary. This eventually becomes a self-feeding cycle which will continually give you more and more time to volunteer for more important tasks.

By establishing yourself as an "Early Riser", being the first person to volunteer for new and difficult assignments over time allows you a level of flexibility as well. Because you are generating a high level of value to the organization more than others, you are also granted a little more leeway than others as well. So, when the time comes that you make a mistake, and rest assured, you *will* make mistakes (You are human after all). Your bosses and supervisors will note that you have a proven track record of having initiative and being willing to take risks. The very nature of taking risks is synonymous with making mistakes. It's expected. I have learned more from my smallest failure than I have from my greatest success. The key is not to make the same mistake *twice*. Learn from it. If you do that when you do make mistakes, your bosses will take note that you are a proven "early riser" and won't take it so seriously if you occasionally "sleep until noon".

This is called earning trust.

Chapter Two

"Like crap through a goose, like shit through a tin horn!"

It wasn't until I turned the age of 18 and joined the US Army as a tanker that I found out the title of this chapter has been famously attributed to General George S. Patton in World War II. Up until that point it my life, I had only ever heard it from my grandfather. So, I will give General Patton his due credit, but it meant more to me coming from my grandfather.

One of the biggest mistakes that people make while working in corporate America is underestimating the value of speed. For those who are unfamiliar with General Patton's famous quote and the meaning behind it, it means fast... VERY FAST.

General Patton has also been famously quoted as stating "A good plan today is better than a perfect plan 3 days from now." This could not be more accurate in the corporate America world. This world is rife with distractions, all day, every day: emails, phone calls, interruptions by customers and co-workers, etc. Employees often will leave their desk to grab something from the printer, or the breakroom and get encountered by several people both on the way to their destination and while returning to their desk leaving them to question what they were originally working on to begin with. The level of inundation can be quite intense. To help save my sanity, and bring a little levity to my day, I created a simple sign to hang up in my cubicle to help me get through the frustration of the interruptions.

The sign was very simple and read as shown below:

TOP TEN WAYS INTERRUPTIONS AFFECT MY DAY

1.

I printed this out on an 11x17 sheet of paper and displayed it for all to see when you first entered my cubicle area. For those that got the joke, it helped them realize what they were doing, and limited some of the noise, but not by much. Most people looked at it, chuckled a little, and then proceeded to interrupt me.

So how can you manage all of these interruptions and

interactions without going crazy. The answer is **speed**. The other element of this is knowing that *addressing* a task, is different than *completing* a task. They are not the same thing. You can address a task, and not complete it. So, what does that mean? Addressing a task can be as simple as reviewing the task to determine how much time, resources, and effort are required to complete it. Bookmarking that time on your calendar in advance and communicating that information to the person or group that assigned you that task in an email or other form of communication.

The key as mentioned earlier, is to do this QUICKLY. Do this as soon as you are assigned the task. This way it is not forgotten about, but also it sets the priority of your workload. If done properly, this shouldn't take more than five to ten minutes. When someone comes up to you with another task that has conflicting deadlines, you can quickly reference the bookmarked time you created, and advise that individual that you are already committed to a different task. Then, you can give the supervisor the opportunity to choose which task is more important. Keep in mind, you are not telling them "No". You are simply stating what you "can do". For example, if someone asks you if you can have a document or task completed by 1pm, instead of simply saying no, you can respond to them with, "I can have it done by the end of the day." More often than not you will find that when you advise people of what you can do, your schedule will fall into line more easily. You won't end up being double and triple booked as much. Most importantly, you will find you're leaving less and less being put off until later.

It may seem tedious at first, but do not put this off until later. Zig Ziglar is a motivational speaker and author who among other things is famously quoted by stating "There is no greater labor-saving tool than tomorrow".

Many people will get tasks assigned to them, and often they will put them off and deal with that issue "Later".

The only problem is that most employees don't have a plan for what to do when "later" arrives. It almost always rears its ugly head at the most inopportune times and forces you to go into a fire-fighting mode and rushing to put together a half-assed effort at the 11th hour just get it off your desk.

If you move quickly when assigned a new task, you have clear visibility of what's on your plate, so you don't become overburdened, and can eliminate the whole fire-fighting process before it even begins.

We've addressed the coordination of the task, but what about completing the task itself. The answer is the same, with speed, but not the way you think.

Most people when they think of speed, see someone moving erratically with intense purpose, often times with reckless abandon, ignoring the consequences of their actions because they are just trying to "Get it done". If nothing else, what I have observed is that when rushing to get a task done more often than not, mistakes are made. Everyone is tasked to do more with less, and everyone has the same deadline, yesterday. So, with taking that into consideration, it can be very easy to see that rushing through something is the preferred method by most people.

These people are missing a very key important detail. Quality. Its long been understood that speed and quality are inversely proportional. Meaning that the faster something is done, the more mistakes can be expected resulting in a lesser quality of the finished product. In my experience when a re-work or error correction was required, we often adopted the satirical slogan of "We do it nice, because we do it twice!".

That is another dirty little secret of corporate America that no one, especially in senior leadership, ever wants to admit. There is always a perpetual crunch of pressure coming down from the higher ups to come in on time, on target, and under budget. No exceptions allowed. When creating these ridiculous parameters, you are creating a scenario where a second trip, or re-work is almost inevitable. They do this because that is what the corporation demands for their shareholders, reality be damned. When reality does inevitably come calling (usually in the form of an irate customer, negative review, or lawsuit for failure to perform) there always seems to be enough time to do the task correctly with all of the resources needed for the highest quality, with no questions asked.

This has been the way of corporate America for decades, and I don't foresee it changing anytime soon. So how do you navigate this terminal loop of incompetence. The answer again is Speed, but as I said before, not the way you think. The key is to quickly focus on the items of the task that bring the highest value with the least amount of work required to complete it. Once that is accomplished you then progressively work your way through to the lowest value task. The important part to remember here is *value*. This doesn't mean it will be an easy part of the task. The highest value portion might be incredibly difficult. Anyone who has been doing a task long enough knows the elements of their task that people care the most about, and also know the mundane details. By taking your time and slowly and methodically addressing those key components of the task you drastically increase the likelihood of success and quality improvement. The key words here are slow but methodical.

So, what does that mean? It means creating a simple, repeatable process, that will help you do the same thing over and over again to the point where you can do it in your sleep. Consistency is the most important part. Consistency is *smooth*, and smooth is *fast*.

By being methodical in your process and how you work through that process, you will find that you may take a little longer than the person who is scrambling through the assignment to get it in early to look good for the boss.

However, when you take into consideration that person is simply preparing a boomerang that is going come back to their desk next week loaded with corrections to be made, and your work will more than likely be approved on the first run, how much time did they really save? The answer is none. The more this occurs, and the more you stay the course, what you will find is that the metrics will show your process is vastly superior, and the bosses will then ask you to share the process, ultimately to become the new company policy on how to do the task. This gives you one more feather in your cap toward the next rung in your climb up the corporate ladder.

This is called time management.

Chapter Three

"He couldn't find his way out of a paper bag with both ends open, a flashlight, and a match!"

Everyone at some point in their time with a company has to work with **that** one co-worker. You know the one that I am talking about. It's that one employee who for reasons beyond everyone's comprehension hasn't, at best, been re-assigned to a more remedial role or at worst, been let go from the company entirely. This is the person who boasts the loudest for the high score on a team project while contributing the least amount of effort. These types of employees are littered throughout corporate America for a multitude of reasons. The biggest reason usually being politics. More often than not some form of nepotism, kids sporting event acquaintance, or something as simple as the boss's friend, etc. is the reason this bad apple is still around.

Not to be crass, but simply being honest, if you haven't immediately identified the employee I'm talking about in your organization by this part of the chapter, keep in mind, it might be you...
This is just a friendly reminder that a little self-reflection from time to time goes a long way.

Most good managers understand that that the quickest way to lose a good employee is to let them watch you tolerate a bad one. Unfortunately, there is a tragic shortage of good managers in corporate America, and for good reason. I'll explain...

I don't believe its hyperbole when I say it's tragic that there is a shortage of good managers. What's worse is that these bad managers not only allow these bad employees to remain in the wrong role, but they often are actually promoted to managers themselves!

For those who haven't worked in corporate America and are dumbfounded by this concept. The explanation is rather simple.

The vast majority of employees who are competent in their role and utilize their common sense can very clearly see that management positions in corporate America are a temporary position at best.

I used to say that when a person takes on a manager's role in one of these large public companies, they are handed a piece of wood. That piece of wood will be turned into one of two things. It will become either a springboard to a higher position in the company, or it will become a plank you walk on your way out the door.

The typical timeline to figure out which one it will be is typically 3 to 4 years. It's for this reason that most sane people who are simply looking to provide for their family avoid these management jobs like the plague due to a lack of job security.

On the flip side of this coin, you have the oblivious employees, who are terrible at their job, have hung around forever despite their incompetence and only see it as an open management position. They also like the idea of moving up in the company. They apply for the job, and more often than not, they get it. This is because it's cheaper to hire from within than paying head hunting firms and recruiting websites to bring in someone from outside of the company. Another reason is the hiring managers naively believe it will increase morale because it shows upward mobility for employees. The entire time being blind to the inner workings of the organization's dynamics of how that new manager will be received by the staff they will be managing. This often provides the opposite result from their intentions. There are some companies out there that do multi-level interviews with potential candidates to determine if they will be a culture fit, but they are incredibly few and far between.

For those employees that don't make it to the ranks of management, they often experience what I like to refer to as "The Screw-up Promotion". In corporate America, it's very rare that an individual employee will ever be taken aside, consulted for their mistakes, given corrective counseling, and then put on a path to help them succeed. More often than not when this type of employee screws up, a broad-brush cowardly policy is implemented for the entire department, branch, etc. that applies to all employees regardless of their performance to show the policy makers bosses that that this mistake will "never happen again".

These policies almost never work. What usually ends up happening is that the poor performing employee in question has demonstrated they cannot do the assigned task. So, as a result of this, the team members who have to work on a daily basis with this person avoid assigning them work of this difficult nature. This is because they don't want to deal with another useless policy that will make their lives that much harder. So that poor performing person essentially just received less work to do, but didn't lose any pay in the process, so voila... I give you the "Screw Up Promotion."

When this type of event happens, I like to call it "Striving for mediocrity". What essentially happens is that you have a series of high performers that consistently produce quality results, and on the other side of the spectrum a bunch of unmotivated clock watchers just waiting for quitting time who rarely produce anything worth mentioning. These blanket broad-brush policies inevitably bring the bottom feeders up in performance, but the collateral damage is that the terrible polices end up bringing the production level of the high performers down at the same time. So, ultimately the good and the bad end up meeting smack dab in the middle. This leaves the company with a mediocre overall performance, perhaps above average at best.

So how do you deal with these employees so that

they don't become bad managers, or get lousy policies created?

The answer is to lead by example. This isn't saying that you need to become the manager yourself. Although if you believe you have the abilities, and the motivation to do so you should consider it.

There is a great quote by one of my favorite authors, Simon Sinek, that applies to how to handle this situation.

 "There are leaders, and there are those who lead" – Simon Sinck

You do not need to be a manager to be a leader. Those who lead are people with a title that carries authority. Yes, that is technically accurate. However, a leader, can be in any role in the organization. Just because someone has authority, doesn't automatically make them a leader.

The best companies and organizations in the world have employees that police themselves. They see an employee who is underperforming or being careless in their duties, and they consult them about their behavior. You don't need a manager to help an employee be better. If you see an employee struggling in an area that you are proficient in, help them out. Don't just tell them what to do. Teach them how to do it. By giving them assistance in building their proficiency you are indirectly helping yourself as well. The better they get at completing a task the less likely you are to be called upon to fix it in the future.

Not only that, if you do aspire to one day become a manager, this will provide you with valuable experience at the ground level that you will be able to pull from in the future should you be encountered with similar situations. Also, because you took the time to show this employee the proper way to do things, they will now have the ability to pay it forward to other employees in the future to help pay it forward as well.

Now, I know this sounds like a utopian rose colored glasses solution for this employee. For some employees, it is. There are some of these unproductive employees that no matter what you do, they will never improve, and they will never be motivated, and they couldn't care less. For those employees that meet these criteria. I would simply say this.

Document it. That is worth saying it a second time. *Document. It.*

In a world of ever expansive human resources departments, it is becoming harder and hard to move on from bad egg employees. If you see an employee who has conduct unbecoming or is putting your organization in a bad light, document it. It doesn't need to be anything more than an email to yourself highlighting the details of the infringement. This way when the opportunity comes to have a conversation with your manager about this employee's performance and how it is negatively impacting the company's performance, you can simply review your email and you will have specific examples with a date and time stamp of the event, and clear detail of the unwanted behavior.

Now I know some people will view this as being a "tattletale" or being a "rat" or "Snitch" by blowing in one of their co-workers. You cannot think that way. You need to view the organization as a whole, not as the sum of its individual parts. For example, let's say this employee was careless in locking up company equipment and $10,000 worth of equipment gets stolen. Do you think that $10,000 is only going to come out of that one employee's paycheck? No, it is going to affect the entire organization's bottom line. That will impact things like raises for everyone else, new equipment or other needed resources that can no longer be purchased because the organization has to replace that stolen equipment. I would be willing to wager that if you gave all of the employees in your organization the option of getting raises and new equipment, or continuing to tolerate a bad employee they would choose the former.

This is not to say that you need to run to your manager every time you see an infraction being committed. What I am saying is that you should be aware of it, and have it documented so that in the event you are questioned by your leadership team you can provide compelling answers.

There is big difference between being accountable and being responsible. The managers and your leadership team are ultimately responsible for the transgressions of the employees in their charge.

As an employee, while you are not ultimately responsible for other employees' actions, you still have a part to play in this scenario. Because you were a witness to these actions, and can provide insight into the unwanted behavior, you have an obligation to provide honest testimony. If you have that information documented, you are not only helping yourself by demonstrating your organizational ability, but also helping your leadership team move on from a bad apple by providing the paper trail required by most human resource departments.

This is called accountability.

Chapter Four

"The hardest decision, and the right decision, are usually the same."

This one-liner that my grandfather shared with me is without a doubt, the single most important bit of advice he has ever given me. I have found this to be true in every single aspect of life. Whether it be at a crossroads at work, in regular life, in a relationship, or any other time when a decision was met with tension on which path to take. This saying served as a compass to always bring me to the best outcome. Keep in mind, that outcome may not have been a good outcome, but it was the best of possible outcomes that could have been expected.

In the previous chapter we discussed accountability. This chapter will take that concept and expand it to the next level. Being accountable is one thing. Being responsible is another. Make no mistake, when it comes to pretty much everything in life, and especially in corporate America, we are not the victims of our circumstances; we are the architects of them. This is an incredibly hard lesson for many people to learn.

Jocko Willink and Leif Babin do an amazing job highlighting the importance of this concept in their book "Extreme Ownership". It is one of my favorite books, and I would highly encourage anyone who hasn't read it, to go out and do so.

When you look at the end result of any decision that is made, there is only one person who is ultimately held responsible for the outcomes of that decision. If you have haven't figured it out yet all you need to do is look into a mirror, and you will see who that person is.

Everyone has the ability to make a decision. Everyone also has the ability to make it right. When it came to making decisions, I always classified the ones that didn't work out into three different categories. Those categories were learning opportunities, mistakes, and trends.

A learning opportunity is exactly as it sounds. More often than not you are attempting to do something for the first time, and to expect instant success is a fool's errand. Very few are great at something from the start. As I have stated before in this book, I have learned more from my smallest failure than I have from my greatest success.

The second category is the true mistake. This is when you have knowledge of what poor decision making will result in. This knowledge was based on past experiences that left you with a familiar and undesirable outcome. These usually happen by accident, or by pure carelessness.

The third category is trends. This is making the same poor decisions over and over again, to the point where you are numb to the results and have begrudgingly accepted the outcome as inevitable. These poor decisions become willful by default or as a product of being overwhelmed by what would be required to make the course correction. The simple term for these trends is called "bad habits".

So why am I focusing on the decisions that didn't go right?

By focusing on these decisions, and their root causes, when you limit them, successful decision making becomes the default, sometimes. It's a hard concept to grasp that successful decisions aren't always intentional. Sometimes it's just dumb luck of being in the right place, at the right time, with the right set of circumstances. For the purposes of this book, I am not spending a ton of time on these types of decisions because they rarely carry the same level of consequences the bad ones do in corporate America. Successful decisions should be celebrated when they occur. The problem is that in corporate America the impact of poor decision making far outweighs any good that was done. I used to always tell my co-workers that it only takes one "Oh Shit!" to wipe out ten "At-A-Boy's." It's very similar to the concept of restaurant reviews. If you go to a restaurant and have a good experience, you will typically tell 2 to 3 people about it. If you have a bad experience, you will tell 10. It's the same thing with corporate America. Talk is cheap when the story is good, and bad news travels much faster than good news.

This is what leads us into the title of this chapter. More often than not in corporate America a decision has been made, and it may not necessarily have been made by you. More often than not this decision was made by someone very high up in the chain of command, and this decision is usually misguided. The usual culprit is a new CEO who has never worked in your industry looking to "shake things up". They have absolutely no idea what you do, only that you aren't doing enough of it, and they are here to "fix it".

Usually, these decisions were made with tunnel vision on the bottom line, with minimal consideration for any other variables.

Unfortunately, that leaves the staff who are responsible for carrying out these decisions with what seems like an impossible task. These decisions typically require staff to forfeit their morals and ethics in order to keep in good standing with the companies' directives or face disciplinary action up to and including termination. Deep down they know that carrying out the decision isnt the best thing for the company or the end user, but what choice do you have, right?

The answer is that you <u>always</u> have a choice. The key is knowing when to make the right decision. That is where the categories I described' above can help you.

If someone issues a directive that you know is wrong, so wrong that you can feel it down in your bones, there really isnt a choice. Is there?

Captain D.Michael Abrashoff, author of *It's Your Ship,* has a great quote that I have found myself referencing often when presented with these types of impossible situations. That quote is simply this:

"If a rule doesn't make sense, break it."

He said this because more often than not the people who made these decisions to begin with have a command-and-control mindset. They don't have the insight to the individual circumstances you are presented with. If they had all of the information you have, they would most likely make a similar decision to yours.

This isn't to say you should be just carelessly going around breaking all the rules that you don't agree with. He did also follow up with the following quote to accompany it:

"If a rule does make sense, break it carefully."

Ultimately what it comes down to is that when you are presented with a difficult decision during your day-to-day activities at work and at life, as the title of this chapter suggests, the hardest decision and the right decision are usually the same.

So, when you look at the situation you are presented with, try as best as you can to compare it to the three categories described earlier as a form of measuring stick to see where your situation falls.

For Example, let's say that you work for a field service organization or a delivery service. And a new decision comes down from corporate that to maximize revenue, the company will now be charging customers not only for the delivery/dispatching fee to their location, but you are now going to also be

charging them a fee for
your return trip back to the
warehouse. Common sense
would dictate that no
customer in their right mind
would be willing to pay this
fee and implementing it
would almost certainly
jeopardize any future
business with that
customer. With that
understanding you have
basically two options. One,
you can invoice that
customer as the company
has directed and be well on
your way to losing that
customer. Or two, you can
waive that invoice fee, and
let the customer know
about the policy, and
inform them you are
waiving the fee because
you value their business.
When the customer sees
what the company is trying
to do, they will almost
always provide feedback
about what a terrible idea
that is, and how they
wouldn't pay it. So, when
your bosses ask you why
you aren't charging this
ridiculous fee, you can
share with them the
feedback from the

customer. If you do this long enough you will have created a compelling business case with documented backup corroborating your position from your customers. That information can then be sent up the chain of command for them to see the folly of their ways, and hopefully guide them to changing the policy. This scenario was an obvious mistake to you, but it is obviously a learning experience for those in charge. Now, if the leadership team receives that compelling evidence that they need to change their ways, and they continue to insist on the policy, well now you have identified a trend. This isnt a learning experience anymore, and clearly a mistake, and officially developed into a bad habit. From here you have some difficult decisions to make. The biggest question is whether or not this issue is worth the fight or is "the juice worth the squeeze".

What I have found is that if
you can provide a
compelling business case
for your decision making,
with documentation to
back it up, more often than
not things will go as you
have articulated. In the
rare instances where you
have a hardheaded
leadership that continues to
pursue a direction that
damages your organizations
reputation, and
compromises your morals
and ethics, you should
consider contacting your
human resources team, or
ombudsman if your
organization has one with
your concerns. If you still
don't see results or least a
compelling explanation of
why these policies continue
to be in place, you may
want to consider looking for
happiness at another
organization that is more in
line with your values.

It's not easy to leave your
workplace, no matter how
bad it is, especially if you
have been there a long
time. I was at a private
organization that ultimately
was bought out and went

public for 15 years. As we got further and further away from being a private organization, the corporate America machine began to take a death grip on the company. It got to the point where the organization that I knew and loved was now a hollowed-out decaying husk of what it used to be. I found that I was loyal to the idea of my memories of what the company was in my mind, instead of what the company actually was in real life. Leaving that company felt like I was disowning a family member and took a tremendous toll on me throughout the decision-making process. When I witnessed compromised ethics and morals for such an extended period of time with no intent to even acknowledge them, let alone correct them, I knew that I didn't want to be associated with that kind of behavior any longer. I had endured enough, and wanted to stand for what was right.

It was an incredibly hard
decision. One of the
hardest decisions in my
career. It was also the right
decision.

This is called Integrity.

Chapter Five

"You could stand on your head, and spit nickels."

I'd like to think that I would
fall into the category of an
overachiever, but in reality,
I'm just a people pleaser
with a strong work ethic.
This one-liner that my
grandfather shared with me
actually didn't have much
to do with my professional
career at first. It was
actually shared with me to
help deal with my father.
My father was an auditor
for the New York State
Department of Labor and
Social Services. As an
auditor his job was to find
stuff wrong for a living.

Unfortunately for me, he brought work home.

It didn't matter how perfect any task or chore was completed, at the conclusion of my assignment the results I provided were never good enough. Sensing my disappointment, my grandfather pulled me aside one day and told me. "You could stand on your head, and spit nickels, and it still wouldn't be good enough." While it sounded funny and was enough to get a 10-year-old to laugh, it cheered me up, but I really didn't know what it meant.

That was the case until I started working in corporate America. Then I got a master class in what that meant. Especially when it came to forecasting. Those who deal with it know exactly where I'm going with this.

This has an impact on private organizations as well, but nothing is more frustrating that the forecasting process for public companies. It doesn't matter if you are forecasting sales booking performance, revenue versus invoicing (RVI), days sales outstanding (DSO), or lag and lead times on a work product. Forecasting is a nightmare. Full stop.

Now in a normal business environment you would look at your traditional run rate or sales cycle that will tell you what amount you could realistically expect to accomplish or turn in a typical month. You would compare this information against your current backlog of work or sales activity, and your historical performance or close rate of what you have typically done in the past. For those who are unfamiliar with this terminology, a run rate is the amount of time or money it typically takes your organization to complete a task or product. A sales cycle is the period of time elapsed from your initial budget quotation to the time the sale is booked.

Now, in most circumstances analyzing this information will generate a relatively reliable forecast that you can confidently provide to your upper management to their complete satisfaction and gratitude with no questions asked.

When you have finished laughing, please continue.

The reality is that no matter what number you provide the answer is unanimously the same across every public company. It's not enough, we need more. For example, let's say your business forecasted a monthly revenue of $500K dollars, but based on the needs of what was promised to Wall Street, the organization requests your forecast to be $700K. So that is your assignment, and more often than not it only sounds like they are asking.

The fact that there isn't any more to provide is

irrelevant. They don't care. Go find it. At least that is the expectation.

More often than not, when employees try to "find" the missing piece of the forecast it is usually pulled from next months expected business. So, for example, let's say your $500K forecast was for June. In order to meet the $700K demand, you need to escalate business originally committed for July, and bring it into June. The unfortunate result of this is that now your July forecast will be $200K below what was originally committed. Upon hearing the news that this month's forecast demands can be met by pulling them forward from next month, the management team showers you with praise and thanks you for saving the month to meet the company commitments to Wall Street. They completely dismiss the information you provided them on where the money came from to fill the Gap. So, when July comes around, your forecast is now not only $200K below what you originally committed to, but they will also repeat the same song and dance as they did in the beginning of June. They raise your originally committed forecast to some unrealistic number in addition to the $200K you voluntarily gave up in effort to help last month's forecast.

It's the corporate America tale as old as time. No good deed goes unpunished. Most forecasting in corporate America follows this path of kicking the can down the road, borrowing from tomorrow to pay for today. This is also known as robbing from Peter to pay Paul. My grandfather also had told me once that "You don't want to rob from Peter to pay Paul, because if you do it enough, you will end up with a sore Peter, and no man likes a sore "Peter"."

Here is the dirty secret that not many people know about forecasting. There is no correct answer. It's a guess, and not even a best guess. More often than not, it's a number that is pulled out of thin air to make one's superiors feel good about their productivity to give the impression of business growth so they can justify keeping their job. That or to show that they are on pace to get their manager a bonus by hitting some unrealistic metric or goal. They are often generated using a year over year model comparing last year's performance to what is expected this year, all the while completely ignoring important information and context. For example, last year's performance may have included a once in a decade sales opportunity that closed this time last year, or extenuating sales bumps like what Amazon, The Home Depot, and Lowes experienced during the pandemic. It's lunacy.

So how can you as an employee successfully approach this disaster waiting to happen. It's painfully clear that any answer you provide will be rejected, increased, and hurled back on you. The answer may surprise you….

Do nothing extra.

Keep your original forecast that you know you can commit to and deliver it. This is MUCH easier said than done. You will get a LOT of push back at first. By pushback I mean heated phone calls from your superiors, a ton of emails, and of course the never-ending supply of spreadsheets and metrics showing how your forecast is unacceptable. This behavior is painfully similar to that of a school yard bully. They are going to make a lot of idle threats in an attempt to get you to react. They are going to get animated, and sometimes unprofessional to try and manipulate you into adjusting your forecast. Don't budge. Just like a schoolyard bully, once they get punched in the mouth, they will learn that their tactics will not work on you, and they will shift their efforts toward another manager, branch or division that is willing to play this stupid game.

Now, you will notice how I said you will get a lot of push back "at first". What I mean by that is you will have to endure this maelstrom for at least a quarter, maybe even two quarters before you will see an amazing transformation in your managers.

By communicating what you know you can deliver, and then delivering that value on a consistent basis, you will see that your managers will stop trying to add targets onto your forecast. They do this for two reasons. One, you have already established that you are not going to play their stupid games and have no interest in the stupid prizes that come with it. Two, they know that the number you are giving them will more than likely come in, so they can use your forecast as a benchmark. Because it is all but certain to come in, it brings a level of stability and reliability into their forecast as well, which helps make them look better in the process.

So, the answer is to do nothing. It is NOT an easy path. But I never said that it would be. It is however the only way that I have found success in navigating this nest of vipers.

I don't mean to sound disparaging to senior level management when I describe these tactics that are used by calling them bullies. But if it looks like duck, and walks like a duck...

If you are a senior level manager reading this book, you should seriously consider looking at the organization through the eyes of your people and how some of these requests can be received. By forcing unrealistic targets on your people that you know full well they won't be able to meet, you are setting them up for failure, and compromising your own integrity and respect they have for you in the process.

In my experience these are not bad people. Just like everyone else they are trying to put food on the table for their families and just working to make it through to retirement. More often than not, the actions that they take are a product of the environment created by the company. This does not excuse the behavior. You always have a choice.

There is a much better way to communicate company targets than just giving employees what I call the "Seagull" Treatment. This is where you walk by their desk, "drop off" some additional work required on their part and just keep on going. That is what typically happens during the forecasting period.

What can be very difficult to navigate during the push back period is when these bullies not only dismiss your forecast but also add the additional target goal to the forecast FOR you.

For example, using our June and July scenario from earlier in this chapter, let's say you properly communicated you would turn $500K and that $700K is not possible. Your manager reads this email and responds with something to the effect of "The number is $700K, figure it out". Hopefully, not in so many words. I would acknowledge that you received the email, double down saying nothing more than "I am committing to $500K. I can't guarantee any more but will try my best." At this point, I would continue on your path to delivering the $500K you said you would commit. When that month end timeframe comes around and your target is $200K short. What you need to do is keep the email exchange where you communicated what you were going to deliver. When your manger comes back and says you missed your forecast. You can confidently state "This wasn't my forecast. It was yours." This is the part where the bully gets punched in the mouth.

The fact that it is documented in an email where your manager wrote a check that your company couldn't cash that is in black and white for all to see. If you can present a solid business case that despite your best effort the best you would be able to turn is $500K, and that $700K is not physically or realistically possible, it will show that you have a greater knowledge and command of your business than your manager does. Even better, let's say you deliver $550K that month. Now, you still fell short of your managers delusions of grandeur, but you have delivered more than you originally committed which shows you were putting your best effort forward.

Make no mistake. Corporations love consistency. Consistency is predictable. Consistency is profitable. If given the opportunity to have volatility in the forecast that will most likely not hit the target but looks good on paper, or consistency which is guaranteed to slightly miss their targets for good or bad, I can assure you they will choose consistency every single time.

The hard part is that it takes a considerable amount of time for you to establish this consistent track record. You need to be able to stack several months back-to-back to create that consistency. Which again is much harder to do than it sounds.

The most important part is to be honest with yourself, so you can be honest with others on what you are able to perform. Even if you have a bad month, and miss

your communicated
forecast, make a business
case to show why it didn't
happen, and when or if you
expect it to happen in the
future.

If you can remain resolute
with the bullies and stay
calm during their barrage of
manipulation, you will be
well on your way to reap
the rewards.

Be patient, it's worth it.
Otherwise, you can stand
on your head and spit
nickels. It won't be good
enough.

This is called under
promising and over
delivering.

Chapter Six

**"We don't see eye to eye,
and it's not because we're
different heights."**

If the last chapter taught us
nothing else, it's the fact
that there are

disagreements and conflict within corporate America. They happen in every aspect of the organization, and they happen often. Whether it be a difference of opinion on how to interpret company policy, company pay practices, or something as simple as how to answer the phone, disagreements are an absolute certainty in your day-to-day life in corporate America.

Picking your battles on which disagreements to pursue can be challenging. Everyone who has worked for corporate America has had this experience. It's early on a Monday morning, you barely got your first sip of coffee and try to settle in for what is bound to be another day of griding through to quitting time. You hear your computer chime that a new email arrived, and lo and behold a new blanket company policy has been rolled out to everyone effective immediately.

More often than not it's a knee-jerk over-reaction to an incident that cost the company a considerable amount of money or got them into hot water and the legal or crisis team is now involved.

One of these incidents that has always been a favorite of mine was one morning when a companywide email was sent from the CEO instituting a new policy where "Any important email must be responded to within 20 minutes".

 Now mind you, this email failed to describe or clarify what is to be considered an important email, or what an acceptable response is, but that is beside the point. You just have better done something within 20 minutes...

This policy was the result of one employee using poor judgement of sending an email to communicate an urgent crisis instead of picking up the phone or communicating it in person. So now as a result, we all must suffer the consequences. Ahh yes, the broad-brush policy once again.

Companies of all kinds have these policies instituted on a daily basis for reasons very similar to this.

Carelessness and apathy play a very large role when these policies are generated. Regardless of the industry, organization, or role within that organization. Almost every one of these policies would not be needed if we utilized one simple tool at everyone's disposal.

Common Sense.

 Common sense has become so rare it should be considered a superpower. When reading these hot off the press policies that come down from corporate the most important thing you can do is try to look at them through the lens of common sense and try to gauge what the intent of the policy is.

More often than not when these policies are drafted and distributed most employees fall into one of four camps.

1. The Oblivious. These are the people for whom the policy was created for in the first place. These are the people who won't read it, wouldn't understand it if they did, and will most likely have this policy used as a paper trail to escort them out the door to find happiness at a different employer.

2. The Compliant. These are the people who may or may not agree with the policy, but they don't want to make waves, so they go along to get along. They begrudgingly follow the policies and whine about it to co-workers behind closed doors or when the boss is not within earshot

when the policy
makes their life
difficult.

3. <u>The Defiant</u> – These
    are the ones who
    no matter what the
    new policy states,
    they know better,
    and they are going
    to do their own
    thing, policy be
    damned. These
    people are the type
    that are
    traditionally only
    happy when they
    are unhappy, so
    battling the dumb
    policy provides a
    twisted sense of joy.
    They will typically
    continue on this
    path until they
    meet their
    inevitable corrective
    counseling
    appointment for not
    drinking the
    corporate Kool-Aid.
    Usually at which
    point they either
    decide to move to
    the compliant group
    or (depending how

important the new
policy is to the
company) move on
to a different
organization.

4. <u>The Opportunists</u> –
This group of
people is where you
want to be. These
are the people who
don't agree with the
new policy but
understand that if
you boil this new
policy down to its
root inception, you
will be able to see
that it was
generated for some
rational purpose.
They try to
determine Its cause
and effect. They
know this policy is a
reaction to an
undesirable event
that transpired. The
opportunists look at
what the policy is
intended to
accomplish and
seek out ways to
meet the intent of
the policy without
having to follow it

to the letter of the law as the policy is written. They seek out this intent by using an important tool. You guessed it... Common Sense.

What's more is that not only will the opportunist group look for the intent, but they also understand that the policy isn't going away, so they will do what the policy makers didn't, and infuse some common sense in how they approach the policy to actually improve it. If it sounds counterintuitive, it's because it is.

The easiest way to get rid of a dumb policy is to embrace it. Embrace it and put your own spin on it to meet the intent and try your best to make it work for you. I

know it can feel
very awkward going
rogue on a new
policy that has been
issued, especially if
you don't agree
with it.

One thing you need
to remember is this,
I'm sure by now you
have found
something in this
book that you can
relate to in your
workplace, and as I
mentioned in the
opening of this
book, all of these
companies are
relatively the same.
It's human nature. I
can all but
guarantee you that
you aren't alone in
your disagreement
with the policy. So,
when you start to
add your
improvements to
the policy that meet
the intent and make
it easier to be in line
than those who are
following it to the
letter of the law.

You will quickly see others witness your actions and begin to follow suit.

What ultimately ends up happening is that your modifications will have turned a dumb policy into at least a functional policy. Eventually that procedural change will make it back to the policy makers, and they will ultimately adopt your methods as the "new" policy. If your name gets attached to it, you could also gain recognition for the improvement and put a feather in your cap to help boost your career path up the corporate ladder as well. The benefits of this don't just end with you either. Hopefully, not only will the policy makers adopt your new policy, but you may also inspire someone else in your organization to put an even better spin on your method making it that much more functional and less frustrating.

Bad policies in corporate America are like the changing of the tide, or a sunrise. It's guaranteed to happen, there's nothing you can do to stop them from being created. All you can do is focus on what you can control. What you can control is how you react to them.

You have the power to choose your attitude on how you react to these productivity killers when they arise.

Remember stress is NOT something that

is done TO you.
Stress is how you
choose to react to
what is being done
to the environment
around you. You
have the ability to
take its power away
and be all the better
for it.

You can choose to
be compliant; you
can choose to be
defiant, or you can
choose to take
advantage of the
opportunity
presented to you.

(if you're oblivious,
you aren't reading
this book)

This is called
Perspective.

Chapter Seven

**"The pocket of excellence –
He's amazing, just ask
him."**

Everyone has or will meet this person. They can do no wrong, their work is perfect, and it's everyone else's fault when things go wrong. You can't have a civil conversation with the person, and they immediately go on the defensive when you try. Sound familiar? In reality, their work is just like everyone else's, flawed. They make mistakes, and more often than not, others are left to pick up the pieces when things go sideways.

My grandfather always referred to these people as a little "pocket of excellence" surrounded by incompetence. He always followed it up by saying. "He's amazing, just ask him."

In the last chapter we discussed disagreements and conflict with policy. Here we will move into a much more complicated area. Disagreements, and conflict with people. Stress has a funny way of bringing out the worst in people. On rare occasions though it can also bring out the best as well. As mentioned earlier in the book, stress is not something that is done to you. It is how you react to the environment around you. I have always followed the philosophy that life is all about how you handle working Plan B, because Plan A never works.

The best way to deal with disagreements is to first know what type of person you are engaging with. You won't be able to know at first glance, but over time and with careful observation of their actions you will be able to understand and anticipate their responses.

To help with these observations, I'd like to share with you a classification system that I have used for years that has helped me in dealing with all walks of life. It's goofy, but it works.

I classify every person I meet into one of three

categories. They are either an egg, a potato, or a coffee bean. You will know which one they are when they get tossed into "hot water".

Obviously, we are not going to be tossing these people into a vat of boiling water (even though you would like to at times). No, the hot water I am referring to is when a project, a task, a decision, or situation has gone breathtakingly wrong. Things like sales missing some critical components on a proposal, the operations team is weeks behind and the client is screaming, production is behind schedule, etc.

These everyday occurrences are barely scratching the surface of the different stressors that corporate America can generate.

So now that we have established what the "hot water" is let's dig a little deeper into the three types of people.

Before I begin, I do want to add this disclaimer. There is no right or wrong personality type. Each person is who they are, and that's fine. I am simply providing these descriptions to help you identify which category each person falls into, so that you can more easily identify whether or not a person's personality type is either in alignment with, or in conflict to the task at hand. You may read these descriptions, and realize that you fall into a group that you don't want to be in. That is also fine.

Self-realization and being honest with yourself is an important part of professional development, and acknowledgement of your own areas of improvement is a great way to start. With that said, lets continue.

THE EGG.

The egg is a person who is mild mannered, typically very quiet, and would be viewed by most as having a soft or kind personality, with a tendency at times to be quick to tears. They also tend to go with the flow, and shy away from making any kind of waves. In other words, fragile.

When the egg gets tossed into hot water you will see that soft and kind composure quickly transform into a hardened exterior putting up a metaphorical wall to keep everyone and everything out. They do their best to mentally isolate themselves from whatever issue or scenario that is creating the stress. They essentially shut down and check out. They become non-responsive to emails, phone calls, and are very dismissive during face-to-face conversations. This is not because they have a problem with you, or the organization, they just "can't deal" with what is going on at the moment.

You should pay attention to when an egg has been assigned to your team in any scenario that involves more than basic administrative or procedural tasks that do not have a clear and concise reaction plan for when things go wrong. This is because this person does their best work when things stay the exact same in a repetitive process with a high margin for error and accountability is scarce.

I don't want to make it sound like being an egg is always a bad thing. Eggs can also provide a benefit to a team when they are utilized in the right role. They are great when it comes to providing a second set of eyes for reviewing completed work, data entry, and administrative work that is not customer facing. Their quiet nature allows them to focus on detail-oriented work without a large number of interruptions for social interaction. They find comfort in the security of a repetitive task. They enjoy knowing exactly what their task is, knowing exactly when their day will begin, and when it will end. They know exactly what is expected of them and meet that expectation. When put in this position to succeed, they can be a model employee. If you put the egg under any kind of pressure though, expect them to crack.

THE POTATO

The potato is a person who is loud and demands attention. They are typically extroverts. They like to talk a good game about how skilled and proficient they are at their work. They give the perception of a stiff upper lip and hardened exterior ready to take on whatever challenge life can throw at them. This is usually because they are insecure in their role in the company and are out to prove to everyone that they need to be assigned the top project or task. They are typically the first ones to respond to email chains volunteering for that top assignment, and also the first ones to complain when they don't get it. The potato likes to talk about their past accomplishments and boast about how thick their skin is handling adversity, and also very quick to provide insight to others on how they should go about performing their job, regardless of whether it was asked for or not.

When the potato gets tossed into hot water, all that talk of a hard surface and thick skin and adversity starts to soften quickly. They come to the self-realization that they have bitten off more than they can chew and knowing full well that they have made a fool of themselves by all of the talk, and too embarrassed to ask for help, they essentially start to melt down into a big pile of mush.

This melt down comes in the form of lashing out at everyone involved in the task, project, or process. They will focus on the smallest mundane detail that helped contribute to the overall failure and over exaggerate the importance of that detail to deflect blame from their own actions. They will not allow themselves to admit when they made a mistake. It must be someone else's fault. These people typically save every email that was ever sent throughout the entire process in the hopes that one of them will serve as a shield to help them deflect the attention.

Once that email is identified, they load up their favorite weapon. The blame-thrower.   At this point all of the information that they could find absolving themselves of any culpability has been fully locked and loaded, and ready to rain down on everyone involved in the process.

Unfortunately, the nature of corporate America is to establish a pay structure that is largely based on a performance bonus/incentive basis. Many companies have setup an environment where ones earning potential puts employees into direct conflict against one another. This is the absolute worst way to build a business, but its reality.

This competitive structure is one of the biggest reasons that you will find more people will fall into the potato category than any other in the corporate America world. They are obsessed with what is known as CYA, or "Cover your Ass" when working as part of a team, and when hot water becomes boiling it turns into CYOA, "Cover your Own Ass" where they will start to throw their own team members under the bus to save their own skin. I don't blame these people personally for behaving that way. Like I have said earlier, I believe that everyone typically shows up to work wanting to do a good job and are just trying to put food on the table to feed their family. I believe that their actions are a product of the environment they are forced to work in.

Much like the egg, the

potato isnt all bad either, as much as it may seem. The potato can play a very important role in team environments. They typically do well when they can run point on a large task, project, etc. when they have a solid support structure behind them. The potato does their best work when they are in roles like sales, project management, and business development. These roles are out in front and operate from the 10,000-foot view looking down. They have the courage to be the first ones in to tackle sticky situations, that would otherwise create a lot of anxiety for others. Their boisterous and outgoing personalities give them the necessary tools to accomplish what few others can. They are willing to stick their noses in the dirt to find out what needs to be done and serve the role similar to that of a musical conductor who makes sure all the necessary instruments are playing when they are supposed to. The potato

really doesn't have any idea
how to perform the task
they are asking for, but they
know when it is supposed
to be done, and what a
good, finished work
product should look like.
They enjoy being the center
of attention when things
are going well which can
help raise morale because
they will talk to the entire
team about how good
everything is going, and
they also like the fact that
they don't need to be the
one to carry all of the
burden should adversity
present itself. The key part
about this person is that
they absolutely need that
support structure. If it isnt
provided, you can all but
expect a mashed pile of
mush after the melt down
happens. This group is
most closely associated
with the "pocket of
excellence".

THE COFFEE BEAN

The coffee bean is a person
who for lack of a better way
to put it, knows what they
don't know. They aren't
overly boisterous, but they

aren't quiet either. They
speak up when they know
their insight will provide
value, or to prevent those
around them from making a
mistake they have
experienced in the past.
They won't make
exaggerated claims about
their past accomplishments
and won't make outlandish
promises on what they will
do in the future. They are
essentially a very "even
keel" type of person with a
very measured and rational
approach to things. They
don't get overly excited
when things go well, and
they don't overly dwell on
their misfortunes when
adversity arrives. More
often than not this person
has a decent amount of
experience in the
organization. You don't
know this by what they say,
you know this by their
actions. They are quick to
respond when they see a
process or task going the
wrong direction, and
typically let others take the
credit for when things are
going well. They are secure
in their role at work and are

comfortable in their own skin mentally. These people are typically your core employees. They are the ones that everyone looks to for guidance, and this is why.

When a coffee bean is thrown into hot water. It remains the exact same consistency it was before it was thrown into the hot water. It doesn't melt down, and it doesn't harden. What it does, is turn the hot water into coffee.

There are many descriptions for this type of behavior the coffee bean demonstrates. Some call it being "cool under fire", some call it being a "Duck on the pond". Others will say they are "Making lemonade" when life threw them lemons. The point is that they acknowledge their situation for what it is. You will often hear them say something to that affect as well. when someone tells you "It is what it is". It's a good indicator that this person knows full well what kind of environment they are in, and they are choosing to not let it affect them. They understand that there are things that are important, and then there are things that they can control. The only things that the coffee bean worries about are the items or tasks that meet both of those criteria. They will focus on the things that are important AND it's something that they have control over. An example of this is having a delayed shipment that is on backorder. It's important, but they have no control over it, so they don't give it much energy. Now, a delayed shipment that is sitting in their warehouse is a different story. It's important, and they can control it, so they act on what needs to be done.

The coffee bean is a person that can be put into almost any role in the organization, and they will figure out what needs to be done. It doesn't matter the personality types they are paired with, or the support structure you provide them, because they will be able to adapt to the situation presented and turn that hot water into coffee.

The good news, in case you haven't figured it out yet, is that you are not doomed to be in one category for your entire career. The stories of the egg, the potato and coffee bean are stories about career progression. Most people when they enter a new organization start out as an egg. They are still learning their new organization and typically keep to themselves until they "come out of their shell" so to speak. Once their confidence builds as they spend time with the organization, they will eventually develop more tendencies that resemble the potato.

After they have had enough time under their belt, they will hopefully learn from the errors of their ways both personally and professionally and develop into a coffee bean to serve as a mentor to others.

Now, that doesn't necessarily mean that everyone will follow this path. Some will be perfectly fine staying as an egg their entire career, and others will be fine staying as a potato. There is nothing wrong with that.

The coffee bean is one who is always looking to better themselves and help those around them. I think it will come as no surprise that most people who read books like this one will fall into the category of coffee bean, or at least will be in the very near future.

The first step toward making your environment into coffee is to identify the team members you are working with and put them into one of the three categories that I described above. Either an egg, a potato or coffee bean.

Now, when it comes to dealing with conflict with these people, please know that you will never be able to remove all conflict. You need to make friends with that idea if you have not already done so. It's just human nature. There are going to be heated conversations with people assigned to work with you. If you can identify which group these people fall into, and work with your management team to make sure that these people are given either the right role on the team, or the right support structure to assist the team that matches their category group, you will be able to drastically reduce the number of opportunities for conflict to even start. In essence you are putting the fire out before it even gets a chance to start.

If a role and responsibility structure is well established at the beginning of the project or process, any conflict that does come up will be easily corrected with little drama. You do this by making sure that each person is matched up to a task that is best suited for what they do well. And if they are being asked to step outside of their comfort zone whether it be due to a lack of workforce, or because you are trying to help groom this person for a larger role in the company, make sure they have a safety net in the form of a solid support structure of people they can contact when they run into an issue. Like everything else we have covered in this book so far, make sure that structure is well documented, and well communicated to all involved.

This is called Teamwork.

Chapter Eight

"If you think you can, or you think you can't, You're right."

My grandfather always told me that "Life was a self-fulfilled prophecy." Now, being a kid, I had no idea what he was talking about. So, when I asked him to explain what he meant by that, he simply told me. "If you think you can do something, or if you think you can't do something, You're right".

I had to stop for a minute to think about that. It's a very powerful statement.

One that too many people are familiar with but fail to truly appreciate it's meaning.

Ultimately what we are talking about is desire. In the last chapter we talked about three different types of people in the corporate world, and the progression between the types. More often than not the key driving factor that determines whether someone will grow in their career or remain running in place at their current role comes down to passion and desire to grow.

Now that may seem like a buzz word to many. It's thrown around all too often in today's society. When you hear someone who disagrees with an assignment or a job they have been given, they often decline the work stating something to the effect that it doesn't allow them to "follow their passion" or they feel like they are not "making an impact". These are the words of someone who is either lazy or lost. When I heard this from co-workers, what I saw was someone who didn't know where they wanted to go in the company. All they knew was that they didn't want to do what they were assigned either. They were in limbo. They suffered from a lack of personal direction.

Passion and desire can be tremendous tools. Unguided passion and desire can be toxic and dangerous.   Let me be clear about this. You do not "follow" your passion. You bring it with you. Much like we discussed in the first chapter of this book, you have the ability to attack each day and volunteer for any opportunity to help you advance, good or bad. The hard part that some people fail to grasp is that sometimes in order to advance in your career you need to take a step backwards. So, what does that mean? By taking a step backwards it could mean taking a pay cut for a role with less responsibility in the short-term that will provide you a more robust path for career growth than the current one you are in. This is especially true if you are in a dead-end job with no upward mobility.

It ultimately comes down to two things. One, having a clear understanding of where you are looking to go in your career. Two, having the willpower and desire to do whatever it takes to get you there. This includes enduring personal hardships like taking a pay cut, working additional hours, working in lousy conditions, extended traveling, and the worst of all... swallowing your pride. People notice when you take a step back, and at times It can come with mockery and ridicule from others.

Going through it sucks. I have experienced that

firsthand. I had worked for a GloboCorp company with aspirations of climbing the corporate ladder. I had made it to the middle management level when it became evident that the sacrifices it would take to move any further would now include a devastating impact to my health because of the amount of stress and pressure the positions above it created. The job itself wasn't where the stress came from. The stress came from the fact that in order to succeed in that corporate world you needed to be able to abandon your ethics and morals to meet company targets. It was the professional version of selling your soul. I wanted to be able to look myself in the mirror when I got up in the morning. I wanted to be someone my family could be proud of. It was already a big ask for them as it was. Abandoning my morals and ethics would be required in addition to the other sacrifices on the altar of corporate America. The altar that had already claimed my personal life. I could never see my family and friends because I was working 80 hours a week.

As I had stated earlier, stress is not something that is done to you, it is how you react to your environment. The knowledge that I had to abandon my integrity and ethics to advance, or even to continue in my current role was tearing me apart inside. My blood pressure was through the roof, and was accompanied by sleepless nights, and endless worrying about the next day being my last because I wouldn't compromise.

It was at this point in my career that I discovered Simon Sinek, and his revolutionary book "Start with Why". The book ultimately forced you to understand the root cause that drives you on a daily basis. The source of your desire and passion.

After reading it and looking around at my surroundings, I realized that my personal goals, and aspirations, combined with how I needed to perform them was not in alignment with why I got into the building system and life safety system industry in the first place.

I wanted to help people. I wanted to save lives and help make the jobs of those people who respond to saving lives that much easier. I wasn't able to accomplish that anymore with this company. My "why" wasn't in alignment with my current organization.

Now you might say, isn't "Starting with Why" and "Following your Passion" the same thing?

Yes and no. I was always passionate about the tasks I didn't like for no other reason than because they were assigned to me. I was determined to do the absolute best I could. I had a clear idea of where I wanted to go in the company, and I worked harder and harder to try and justify how the tasks I was assigned fit into the reason "Why" I was doing the tasks in the first place.

This was right up until the point where it would cost me my health to continue. That was one sacrifice I was not willing to make.

I had a small startup company that had been attempting to recruit me for some time that I had respectfully declined to join on multiple occasions. The pay would have been less, and the work would have been more. I had looked at it as an overall "lose – lose" situation prior to reading "Start with Why".

When the opportunity came around again to work with this company, I realized that I could continue on my path of career development, in the same industry, but this time, having the ability to tailor the company to what I thought it should be because it was a startup with little to no processes or procedures in place.

I had been at the GloboCorp company for roughly 15 years, and it was all I had ever known at the time. The thought of leaving was terrifying. I had become comfortable with the "Devil I Knew". It took a considerable amount of self-realization and inner reflection of what was happening to me to finally realize that the only thing that was more terrifying than leaving, was staying. It was only a matter of time before I would lose my job due to a reduction in force to meet the company's bottom line. Middle management was always the first to go, regardless of how good or bad you performed. The only people who were relatively safe were revenue generating positions, and I was already a prime candidate to cut because I wouldn't play ball.

So, I made the leap of faith, and joined the startup company. This was one of the single most impactful decisions I had ever made for many reasons.

I woke up after my last day with the GloboCorp company, and the sun still rose in the morning, the birds were still singing, my friends that I had there still spoke to me. It was a very awkward feeling. One of both freedom and despair at the same time. "What have I done?" I thought to myself. I left a huge corporation with all of the resources in the world, a never-ending list of sales opportunities and the workforce to complete the task for the complete unknown.

It was overwhelming at first. The sentiment washed over me like a dirty puddle of pothole water being splashed all over me by a passing truck as it hit the pothole.

"I'm all alone... What do I do now?"

"I don't know if I can do this..."

"Can I do this?"

These thoughts were racing in my head almost constantly. I had been living such a structured life working 80 hours a week for years on end. Get up, go to work, come home with just enough time to eat something before crashing on the couch and going to sleep. Waking up at 1 or 2 in the morning, and then going to bed.

Rinse, and repeat.

Day in and day out, every day for 15 years. Now all of a sudden having so much time on my hands, I felt almost like a fugitive on the run. Out in the frigid cold wilderness, except there was no going back, and no one was coming looking for me.

I had been looking for guidance everywhere on how to proceed, because this was completely foreign territory to me.

One story that came to my attention that provided some semblance of inspiration was the story of Hernán Cortés. He was a famous Spanish conquistador who was tasked with Spanish conquest of the Aztec Empire in Mexico. When his ships landed ashore, he notoriously set the ships on fire so that his men knew that there was no escape or going back, and failure was not an option. Whether the men wanted to be there or not, they didn't have a choice anymore.

In trying to find some less brutal form of inspiration I also came across the book "Think and Grow Rich" by Napoleon Hill. This book highlighted the benefits of desire, and what could be done to harness its power. I won't go into the details about the book, because I don't want to spoil it for anyone, but I would highly recommend it to anyone.

Even though I was on my own, and I could only rely on myself. I came to understand there was no better person in the world for me to rely on.

This was because I was the only person in the world who truly knew what I was capable of accomplishing. I knew that I couldn't fail.

While I didn't burn any bridges when I left the GloboCorp company, I didn't make any new friends either in the process.

I had to succeed; I had no choice. There was no going back in my mind. No matter what adversity was presented to me, I needed to find a way to adapt and overcome the obstacles.

Now, you may not be presented with the same extenuating circumstances that I was, but rest assured you are all that you need to stay on the path to reach your goals. You just need to believe in yourself. Remember, whether you think you can, or think you can't...You're Right.

This is called perseverance.

Chapter Nine

"They're so cheap that they're tighter than two coats of paint!"

My Grandfather loved to haggle when it came to pricing on things. Always trying to get as much value from things as he could. Especially when it came to buying new cars. Whenever someone came to him celebrating how much they saved on a purchase off from the list price he would always respond with a devilish smile and soul crushing quip of "So what's it worth?" Whenever my grandfather couldn't successfully haggle with someone on price or find a cheaper way to do business with someone, he would always say that person was so cheap that they were "tighter than two coats of paint."

Whether you are embarking on a new career adventure like I was with a startup company, or if you are just looking to sharpen your financial performance in your current organization, everyone is ultimately confronted by the same villain. The dreaded profit and loss (P&L) statement or budget.

When topics like earnings before interest, taxes, and amortization (EBITA) come up in corporate America, you can count on several things to happen. The administration team groans, the accountants get wide-eyed, the operations team anticipates not getting the resources they requested, and the sales team's eyes start to glaze over as they drift off mentally to think about their golf game.

Simply put, It's not a popular topic.

Unfortunately for everyone, it's also one of the most important topics.

That's the truth of it all, isnt it? In the corporate America world, every organization is "tighter than two coats of paint". Do more and more, with less and less. This forces everyone from the rank and file all the way up to senior leadership to be ever observant on ways to be more efficient in their work practices. This includes getting the most life out of existing equipment, recycling and reusing as many consumables as possible, reducing waste, and tightening up work procedures to streamline the amount of workforce time on task. Some things never change. It's all about the bottom line.

It's the reason everyone is in the room to begin with, like it or not.

When I left to join the startup company, I found myself leaving an environment that was essentially the land of unlimited resources, to one that now could be considered a barren desert, by comparison.

My funds were low, my debts were high. I needed to become more efficient in how I operated if I was going to succeed.

It was around this time that I discovered a great book by Capt. D.Michael Abrashoff titled "*It's your Ship* –

Simon Sinek's "*Start with
Why*" helped inspire the
vision of what I was looking
to accomplish. Capt.
Abrashoff's book provided
the "How" required to
accomplish that vision. I
have such a deep respect
for these authors that I
don't want to give away all
of the details in these
books, but I would highly
suggest you read them.
They changed my life.

The answer on how to
accomplish your vision was
a lot simpler than most
people realize.

He made it a point to
interview every single
person in his organization
to gain carnal knowledge of
each person in his
command. To learn their
likes and dislikes, and what
they enjoyed about their
current roles, and what
they wanted to do in the
future.

I followed many of the
guidelines that were listed

in this book, but the most important one I took from the book is to be an aggressive listener. Listen to your people and see the organization through their eyes.

My grandfather used to say, "You have two ears, and one mouth…use what you have more of."

Many corporations today in efforts to fatten the bottom line are quick to cut labor or what is commonly known as a reduction in force, or RIF. Depending on the industry you are in, there is almost always a slow time of the year, and you can almost guarantee that when it comes close to the deadlines for reporting to Wall Street about quarterly earnings that some co-workers will be on the outside looking in whether they deserved it or not.

Instead of cutting those valuable people, especially in a day and age when finding qualified help is at a premium. Organizational leadership should be listening to them.

We have discussed broad brush policies earlier in this book, and my disdain for them. The one thing that we didn't discuss was something even worse.

Ancient Policies. These are the traditional policies that are followed because "We've always done it this way."

I can't tell you how many times I've heard that response when raising questions about policies that are outdated and as old as the hills.

Make no mistake the words "We've always done it this way." or any variation to the like are hands down the most expensive words in the English language.

Corporate leadership typically sends down a command-and-control policy for the rank and file to follow in the hope and intent that it will improve the bottom line. In reality, those policies are lacking clarity, poorly communicated, and rarely understood if they are even received at all.

What ends up happening is that you have a select few in the organization that are able to somewhat determine what the intent is and find a better way to do it. The corporate leadership sees the numbers are going up, so they think it's the policy they sent out working successfully, and the remaining divisions, departments, branches, etc. that don't hit targets are just not following the policy correctly.

The better way to approach this is to sit down and genuinely listen to your rank-and-file workers who are doing the hard work and listen to what they have to say. Even if you aren't the manager. More often than not they will be able to provide you with the elements of the policies that have absolutely no value to the organization, despite what the policy may claim. They will be able to show you new tools they discovered, or process tweaks they created to speed up the process.

By empowering these people to find new and creative ways to accomplish the company's goals, instead of just towing the "We've always done it this way" line, you will set yourself up for increased profits by the labor savings alone.

The fact that you gave the employees the opportunity to provide insight and feedback into the company will also help them feel more valued and give them the sense that they are "Making an Impact". It will raise morale and inspire other employees to see what ways they can come up with to be more efficient.

Now, will all of their ideas be good? No. They won't. In fact, some of their ideas will be downright terrible. But that doesn't mean you shouldn't do it anyway. By empowering your employees to be involved in the execution of your processes and giving them the opportunity to fail, you will see them take a greater ownership in their daily tasks. This is because their name is now associated with what's happening. It's not just some large faceless company vomiting bad policy down on them.

One example I can give you is this lesson I learned. In the battle of supplies versus labor hours, supplies will win every single time.

I had heard from multiple employees that the tools we were providing them to perform their work were inferior in quality and it took them twice, sometimes three times longer to complete a task than If I had spent an extra $2,000 per person to give them the quality tools they requested.

I listened. I went out on a limb and purchased the tools for our staff, which was roughly a $16,000 direct hit to my bottom line that month. Much to my surprise every single job for the remainder of that month, as well as every job since came in at almost half the labor that was originally proposed. That labor savings not only paid off the $16,000 for the tools I bought, but provided a labor savings that was so far ahead of budget that I was able to add even more tools than what was originally requested. I made sure all of the leadership team, and everyone in the field knew that the suggestion of the tools came from our field staff, and that they should get all the praise for our financial successes that year. Our ownership team ultimately provided them with financial bonuses for the great idea, which was a rare thing for hourly employees at this company.

Having an open and interactive conversation with my staff led to many examples of situations like this where they would simply run into an issue with a policy or a procedure and start the conversation with a simple question:

"Why are we doing it this way?"

I would take a moment and look into our current policies and procedures that were issued to us. If I spent 5 or more minutes researching it, and I couldn't come up with any kind of compelling answer to end the conversation, I made a vow to do the following:

I would sit down with that employee who asked the question, and we would draft a new way to accomplish the task.

I explained to the employee, I want you to picture in your mind a football field. On that field are two large white out of bounds markers on each side of the field.

One out of bounds marker was that you are going to damage our organization's reputation. Meaning that any solution that would question our morals, ethics, professionalism, or employee's safety was off limits.

The second out of bounds marker was that it was going to cost the organization some ridiculous amount of money to implement it.

As long as it was within those two out of bounds markers, and it made good business sense to the both of us, we were going to roll with it. But here was the catch. Seeing as that employee is the one who came to me with the issue, and helped draft the solution, that employee now shared ownership in that process, and was responsible for making sure that his fellow co-workers were abiding by the policy.

By doing it this way, it helped raise the accountability of our staff because they now had some "skin in the game", or ownership of the process because their name was attached to it.

Because it was being spread by word of mouth, and not just by email or phone call it was a constant topic that was brought up in passing conversations.

Other employees saw that one of their coworkers was able to influence how the organization was run and started paying closer attention to how they could improve things as well.

And last but certainly not least, because the employees were involved in helping create these policies, they ended up self-policing them when they saw some of their co-workers stepping out of line or cutting corners that went against what was agreed upon. Because the employees were self-policing each other, it freed up time for me as the manager to focus on more important tasks like growing the business instead of having to sit down with employees for disciplinary discussions.

What was great about it as well, is that it became a fun competition for the employees to come up with new and creative ways to be more efficient in their roles. They knew if they could make a solid business case, they would be able to get higher end tools, better working conditions, and much more.

Now, I wish I could say that every idea that came to me was a brilliant one and we made a ton of money on them, but that wouldn't be accurate. We had some ideas that were flat out duds, and never got off the ground.

After a while I started paying attention to the ideas that were coming in, and seeing which ones were successful and which ones were going to crash and burn. It didn't take very long to identify a trend that was happening between the results. What I discovered in the ideas that ultimately ended up failing is that it wasn't that the idea was bad, it was how that idea was delivered and implemented.

Remember how I said the employee that came with the question was the one that had to deliver and enforce the policy?

Well, it turns out that a good idea is only as good as how it's delivered to the recipient. I was at times shocked to see that what I though was a great idea was ill received by the staff and ultimately ignored sending us back to the drawing board.

When I went to observe how the message was being relayed to their fellow employees what I essentially saw was a 3-Star Michelin meal being served on a garbage can lid.

The content was outstanding, but the delivery was absolutely abysmal. The employee would essentially just tell others about it instead of teaching or explaining to them why it was important. It came across to the other employees as If they were being given orders from a peer. Which went over about as well as a fart in church. It was no wonder that these ideas were ending up dead on arrival.

When I looked at the employees who had successfully conveyed their policy ideas to the team, I noticed something completely different as to how it was received by their coworkers. They all had different ways of going about it, but the same ingredients or components were there.   Any successful policy to save costs had to have these three elements to it.

1. It needs to be simple.
2. It needs to be easy.
3. It needs to be convenient.

I have long said that every single person on this Earth listens to the exact same radio station. WII-FM (What's in It for Me) When you are asking someone to go out of their way to do something new, the natural human instinct is to resist change. So, when it is conveyed to people in a way that is simple, easy, and convenient you are less likely to encounter resistance.

I want to dig into this a little bit deeper because its an important topic and it requires some clarification. Just because something is simple, doesn't mean its easy. Just because something is easy, doesn't mean it's simple. Just because something is simple and easy, doesn't mean that its convenient.

Clear as mud, right?

Let me explain with an example of what I am talking about:

Winning the lottery is *simple*. It's not *easy*.

Completing your taxes is *easy*, it's just not *simple*.

Completing your easy taxes after simply winning the lottery is not convenient.

The easiest way to determine if your policy is simple, easy, and convenient is to try and explain it as if you were talking to a 5-year-old. Now I am not trying to insult the intelligence of our co-workers by calling them 5-year-olds, I am simply making the case that if you can have complete understanding and command of a policy to the point where you can explain it in the simplest of terms, most people should not have an issue getting on board with the decision.

Here is a real-world example of what I am talking about. I had worked for a field service company that required periodic safety meetings to be compliant with OSHA. The company prior to my arrival had always conducted these meetings in the afternoon, they had always done it this way. Their thought process was that the employees would come in at the end of their day, turn in their paperwork for the work completed that day, and then attend the meeting.

When looking at it in depth. A big reason that they had the meetings at the end of the day was more about a lack of trust that the employees were working a full day, and it was a way to verify that they were putting in a full day's work.

No one liked it. The meetings always ran late. Not only did the safety meetings run long because we had to pull people from customer sites to return to the office, but we also were paying them for that travel time back to the office and also for any overtime that was spent to cover the required safety content.

The new policy that was communicated out was that we were going to move our safety meetings to the mornings.

Employees always knew that their first stop of the day was going to be the office for a safety meeting. (Simple)

Because they hadn't gone to any customer sites yet, there was no paperwork for them to file when they arrived. (Easy)

Because they had customers sites to be at, the meetings didn't run long. Also, more often than not, they were able to get

home a reasonable time.
(Convenient)

From a P&L aspect of this.
Employees commute to the
office was on their personal
time, so we saved the
money we had previously
been paying for them to
travel back to the office.
Because we moved these
meetings to the morning,
we didn't have to pull
employees from the field so
they could stay on site
performing billable work.
The best part of all, is that
because the meetings never
ran long, and they were in
the mornings we never had
to worry about paying
overtime for wages we
couldn't bill for, and the
employees were happy
because they didn't have to
stay late.

This all started because an
employee raised the
question of why we are
always sitting in this
conference room waiting
for people to return from
jobsites.

 Be an aggressive listener. It
is worth your time and your
bottom line will thank you

for it. This way you won't have to be "tighter than two coats of paint".

This is called empowerment.

Chapter Ten

"If you threw them out of a window, it would take a week to hit the ground!"

One of the things that always amazed me, and not in a good way, was how long it took corporations to make a basic decision or approval. This included everything from the initial offer letter issued to a new hire after the interview, to basic payroll processing, all the way to something as simple as responding to an email request. This is more of an issue with public corporations and public entities than it is with smaller private industries. In the corporate America world, the larger the company the longer the wait. When it came to a change or approval of anything at the GloboCorp company I worked at, as my grandfather would say: "If you threw them out of a window it would take a week to hit the ground!"

Now obviously the laws of physics would prove that to be impossible but that doesn't make it any less accurate. If a new change or policy was passed by the CEO, and a change had to be made across the board, the organization had the turning ratio of a battleship. Sadly, that isn't even the worst of them all. If you end up in the public sector working for the state or the federal government, the time you will wait in corporate America will seem like a New York minute.

You get the point, there is a lot of waiting required when dealing with public organizations. Sometimes for good reasons, most of the time it's not. But nevertheless, here you are waiting.

Most of the time that we spent waiting had to do

with the fiscal cycle and where on the fiscal calendar year our request fell in contrast to when reporting would be due for Wall Street. It didn't matter how essential or urgent the need for equipment or supplies were. If the company hadn't yet posted its earnings to Wall Street, the answer was no, and you had to wait.

Conversations when walking into the boss's office were usually cut short or came to a very abrupt ending. Usually, they would go something to the effect of:

Employee: *Good morning Boss, Is it possible to…*

Boss: *No, (cutting the employee off mid-sentence) now what did you want?*

Employee: *We can talk about it next quarter.*

Once the reporting was completed you were free to open requisitions for new hires again or order that large equipment expenditure you had asked for 2 months ago.

In the last chapter we talked about helping our bottom line by implementing some policy and procedural changes that came through the eyes of your people.

In smaller private companies its very easy to make those changes and move quickly to implement them.

In larger public companies, not so much.

There is a Ying and a Yang to almost every aspect of life.   In a smaller company, you don't have same resources as the big outfits, but you can move quicker. That is the tradeoff.

In a large public company, you have all the resources you could ever want, along with some that you wouldn't wish on your worst enemy. Like bureaucracy.

You know your business like the back of your hand, you know what is needed, why its needed, and when it's needed. So go ahead and get it done. In most businesses that would be enough.

In corporate America you need to pass decisions like this through someone with a made-up title like the Executive Vice President of Coffee Drinking. I actually had that nickname coined for one our VP's because I had no idea what he did, but that is all I ever saw him do. As stated earlier, they have no idea what you do, they just know that you aren't doing enough of it.

So, when you have a good idea from one of your employees, or a new policy needs to be rolled out, or you have an urgent equipment purchase required what are you supposed to besides wait?

In my experience what I have found is that it is easier to ask for forgiveness than it is to ask for permission. I know that this sounds like you are going to be on the fast track to meet up with Human Resources. I'm sure you can already envision it as they are preparing your pink slip and your walking papers. Believe me when I tell you that you're wrong. It's a sound philosophy, when used properly. You just want to make sure that you are able to provide a compelling business case for your decision making. When first starting out using this tactic, be sure to use it sparingly.

Now, the key to this process is to continue following the established process as it is written. Send the email, phone call, or online process that you would normally follow to accomplish your task in question. After you do that, go ahead, and implement what you were looking to do. This tactic works best when you know you have a considerable amount of time before you will get an answer from your organization's headquarters. My typical reference guide is if I have any decision or approval where I know I will be waiting longer than a week to get an answer, I am going to move forward with it regardless.

The reason I say that, is because I know most good ideas in a crisis, or urgent requests that come up will need to be implemented or addressed in less than a weeks' time.

This way by the time the decision comes back from the coffee drinking VP, no matter what the ruling is, the issue is already resolved. The VP can continue to do nothing because that person is in a win-win situation. The action has already been taken, and if necessary, there is a person to blame if it goes sideways. If the decision you made, that he *"approved"* works out, he looks incredibly efficient in the turnaround time from decision to execution. More importantly you have now established a precedent that will allow you to follow a similar action to this type of issue in the future. It also helps you establish and build trust with that VP where he will be less likely

to question your decision
making in the future.

This is the reason that I say
you should use this tactic
sparingly, and never on the
same issue twice when
starting out. If you follow
these guidelines, and your
idea does unfortunately
end up going sideways, you
can claim ignorance to the
policy while still trying to do
the best for your
employees and customers.

The other tactic that you
can use is to treat the
organization response time
as if they were a
manufacturer with a
backorder. You know that
they are going to take on
average, let's say 2 weeks
to approve a request. If
you have visibility of the
need ahead of time,
request it 2 weeks early so
you can remain
streamlined. On rare
occasions companies will
get wise to this, and
eventually come and give
you a slap on the wrist, but
most of the time they are
so overwhelmed, or blind
to everything that moves

where no one will notice that your staging requests were submitted in advance.

The key to this tactic working is to think like your boss. Get in their head with their priorities and objectives. More often than not in a public organization the priority and objectives are almost always centered around the shareholder. So, if you can find ways to obtain things in a cheaper faster method without sacrificing quality, more often than not no one will give you much grief. For example, when I had to wait for material procurement policies to be executed which could sometimes end up taking 2 to 3 weeks to fulfill, I would look at outside sources like Grainger, or Amazon, or some other 3rd party site that had the same material I needed. It wasn't technically on the "Approved" vendor list that the organization had established terms with, but it was the same part, usually much cheaper, and I could have it in a quarter of the time. I found a way to meet the quality standards, while saving time, and material costs for the company, while keeping our clients schedule on time. Did my accounting team get their feathers ruffled because they had to process a 3rd party invoice? Absolutely. But when they saw while processing the invoice that it resulted in a savings, they changed their tune pretty quickly.

What you want to do is think like your boss, but unlike your boss, learn your organizations system inside and out. By system I don't mean computer software, although that may be the case in your specific circumstances. By system I mean the ins and outs of how the processes work at your organization. It may be a combination of computer software, with hand offs between staff members, or a tiered approval process that needs to go up the corporate food chain, etc..

The point is that every organization has their

"system" that they use for processing administrative work. The key to avoiding the limitations of the system is to have communications with all the different people who have an interaction with the system for what you are looking to accomplish. Sales, Operations, Administrative, Accounting, logistics, etc.

It doesn't need to be any kind of long communication either. When possible, pick up the phone, hit them up on a virtual call, or stop by their desk. Ask them about what pain points they have in the system.

Yes, you read that correctly. I am instructing you to go talk to your co-workers and ask that they complain to you.

As mentioned earlier in the book. If you go to a restaurant and have a good experience, you will tell two to three people, where if you have a bad experience, you will tell ten. That is just human nature. People LOVE to complain. Venting makes

us all feel better. More
importantly when you
invite the grievances, you
will get a more honest
answer from them than if
you asked them what they
like about the system.
When you ask for positive
feedback about something,
people will more often than
not tell you what they think
you want to hear.
Especially if the person
asking the question is in a
leadership position. This
can also be true when
asking about problems with
the system. Some people
don't want to come across
as "complaining" because
they feel it will negatively
affect how you view them,
and they don't want to
come across as a person
making waves. Self-
preservation is human
nature as well.

That's why whenever I had
these conversations with
people, I would usually start
the conversation with a
pain point that I was
experiencing, and then
would ask them if they
were experiencing a similar
problem.

I would start off the conversation with something like "Hi, did you notice that the system seems to be taking forever to generate a purchase order number? Are you experiencing that too, or is it just me?"

By starting off my conversation asking for their help, it makes them feel involved, and important. Also, because I opened the door to complain about the system, they are more likely to walk through it and join you in the conversation.

From here you can start to have a candid conversation with them about the limitations of the system your organization uses, and where to find the "Cracks" that most requests seem to fall into at the most inopportune time.

Things like a form field that was missing or incomplete that the system required. Something so simple would bring the entire process to a screeching halt until the information required was provided. This combined with the fact that nobody typically lets anyone know about the missing information because its "not their job" has the request sitting in limbo until it becomes a crisis. Only until someone asks why it wasn't done yet does someone do the digging and find out that this request was in limbo for weeks.   Sound familiar?

So, by doing this with each department or staff member that interacts with the system that you use, you can begin to see the bigger picture of how things work. Even better you get to see what is important to THEM. By viewing the process and how it flows through their eyes, you can pay attention to those pain points for each person who contacts your request to make sure that they never have to experience that issue with you.

By doing this with consistency, people will come to know that your paperwork requests will

typically be accurate
enough to not create any
stress or anxiety for them
and will be moved to the
top of the line. Once again
human nature at its finest.
People like to take the path
of least resistance. It's a
seldom few that want to
tackle the headaches first.
(even though that is the
right approach).

Because those annoying
speedbumps are removed,
those people will more
often than not overlook any
mundane details that don't
really have anything to do
with your request.
Everyone knows that they
are essentially checking a
stupid outdated box that
was put there by some
blanket policy five years
ago as a result of one
person's bad decision, and
never removed.

This may not streamline
your organizations process
to blazing speeds, but what
you will find is that the
normal eternity you end up
waiting for is drastically
reduced to half, sometimes
three quarters of the time.

Unfortunately, you will never be able to eliminate all waiting. However, if you can think like your boss, and see the system through the eyes of the people who use it, you will at least be able to actively pass the time while you are waiting for them to "Hit the ground."

This is called building relationships.

Chapter Eleven

"Knowledge is knowing a tomato is a fruit. Wisdom is knowing you don't put it in a fruit salad."

In the previous chapter we discussed building relationships. Part of building relationships is understanding the people you are trying to build them with. Life can be a 4-letter word at times and each person has their own personal challenges and struggles they deal with. More importantly, each person needs to traverse their own path at their own pace. For some navigating this path comes easier than it does for others. Some people are naturally street smart, and others are naturally book smart. Both types have their own unique set of advantages and disadvantages. There is no right or wrong way to walk this path because it is unique to the individual.

I will be the first person to tell you that you need to walk a mile in that person's shoes before you tell them how to tie their laces.

Traditionally, the path of book smarts is considered to be the path of knowledge. Conversely, the path of street smarts is more aligned with the path of wisdom.

My grandfather always told me that "Knowledge is knowing that a tomato is a fruit. Wisdom is knowing that you don't put it in a fruit salad."

With that understanding, a key element to be aware of

in corporate America is
being able to identify which
path a person is on and
make the determination if it
is a path to join, or to avoid.
Let me explain.

A very hard truth, that
some people will have a
hard time accepting is this.
Knowledge and intelligence
are not the same thing. Not
even close. There are many
people who have spent a
considerable amount of
time, effort, energy and
especially money obtaining
high end college degrees.
These include a Bachelors
(BS), Masters (MS or MBA),
and a Doctorate (PHD).

These people have decided
to forgo real world
experience to have more
time in the classroom.
Which in some professions
is a pre-requisite for a job,
or for a promotion. It's
hard to blame them in
those instances, especially
if their employer is willing
to pay for them to obtain
the degree. Who wants to
say no to a free education,
right?

But is it really an education? There lies the question. The answer, along with the devil, is always in the details. Mark Twain is famously attributed for the following quote:

"Don't let schooling interfere with your education." – Mark Twain

While they do gain an extensive amount of knowledge in the classroom, the amount of information obtained in comparison to the amount of information that is used in practical applications in corporate America is very little. More often than not, the 3 letters after their name serves no other purpose than to get them an interview. In today's society applicants with an MBA are so common the accomplishment itself is taken for granted.

The people in corporate America who have been working at the company for a while typically know the ins and outs of how the company works. When they see a new hire coming in the door or a person being promoted who goes out of their way to tell you that they have an MBA or a PHD, it's typically seen as a *red flag.*

They immediately acknowledge that this person should be kept at a distance. This is until they can prove, using real world applications, that they know what they are doing, and that they are more than just a degree.

These people who go out of their way to announce their accolades have a misplaced sense of pride in their accomplishment. This is not to say that they are bad people, or that they shouldn't be proud of their accomplishment. To further clarify the point, I think it's great that people choose to better themselves and improve their station in life, just don't rub people's noses in it.

Unfortunately, these people typically use the degree to serve as a shield that they use to hide their insecurities about their ability to perform the new role. They go out of their way to tell you how much knowledge they have in hopes that you will take it at face value, and not probe any further. The problem is that it has the exact opposite affect from the one they desire. When they bring it up, the person on the other end of the conversation sees them as condescending and pretentious. Almost as if the new hire was talking down to them because they haven't reached the same level of accomplishment. Listening to the person boast about the degree makes the listener feel as though they are viewed as a commoner.

Now, I don't want to paint the picture that everyone who has a graduate or advanced degree is a blithering idiot. Please don't read it the wrong way. The people that I am referring to are the ones who go *out of their way* to tell you about their degree. This isn't something that comes out of organic conversation. This is a topic that is manufactured and injected into the conversation to gain attention.

A perfect example of this was a commercial spot that FedEx ran in 2006 to promote how easy their new shipping website was to use. The commercial opened with a supervisor frantically approaching their new hire, Tom. She said, "I know it's your first day, but we really need your help, because we are in a bit of a jam." Tom gets up from his desk and puts on his freshly pressed sport coat and takes a quick shot of breath freshener spray in a confident manner with a slight grin. As they fervently walk down the hallway to the warehouse, they enter the room with boxes as far as they eye can see stacked from the floor to the forty-foot ceiling. She turns to him and states that "All of this has to get out today." At which point he raises both hands, and states to her using a downward inflection tone that "Yeah…. I don't do shipping." She responds to Tom in an assuring manner by saying "Oh, no, no, no, its very easy we use FedEx.com, anybody can do it." At which point Tom responds with a tilted head and a disappointed smirk. The kind a parent would give a child when they caught them in a lie, and states in a condescending tone "you don't understand… *I have an MBA.*"

The supervisor takes this comment in stride, takes a moment to collect herself, and professionally responds with "Oh, you have an MBA…. In that case I am going to have to show you how to do it."

To which the commercial closes with the narrator giving the tagline of "FedEx.com it's so easy, even an MBA can do it."

This is the same treatment people experience when PHD graduates interrupt you in mid-sentence because you didn't refer to them as "Doctor" when addressing them instead of Mr. or Mrs., or sir or madame.

What you would like to say to them is okay pal, if you're on a plane and someone screams out "Is there a doctor on board!? Are you going to stand up to assist?" The vacant stare you get as a response is worth its weight in gold.

My personal favorite response to such a *"magnanimous"* individual is to explain to them "You know I've found the problem with being better than everyone else, is people seem to think you're pretentious, what are your thoughts?"

As much as you would like to respond with one of these sayings and put them in their place, don't do it. Be the bigger person and give them the respect that they decided you didn't deserve, and know that if they continue with that kind of behavior, they won't last long. It may feel good to get a shot in at their expense, but in the long run it will only hurt you. Their actions and comments say much more about them than they do about you. Don't let your ego become your undoing.

I am not trying to completely belittle anyone with an MBA or PHD, I am just trying to drive home a simple point. When you step foot in that new corporate America office on Day 1, you have accomplished exactly this:

Nothing.

You have proven nothing to your staff, nothing to your bosses, and nothing to your clients. As far as they are concerned you are the equivalent of a green horn on a crab fishing vessel like the ones depicted on Discovery's *Deadliest Catch*. Like it or not, you're a rookie. This goes the same for industry veterans starting at a new company. When you boast about accomplishments on day 1, everyone will believe they need to keep an eye on you to make sure you don't get them or yourself into hot water. This is until you can prove otherwise.

I always used the following guide to help determine how much of the information that came from these people was useful, and how much to ignore:

BS – Bullshit

MBA- Master Bullshit Artist

PHD – Piled High and Deep

Now, I don't want to sound like a complete hypocrite, because I do have two bachelor's degrees. I will be the first person to tell you that they didn't really do much for me. They didn't even get me in the door. I was able to hire on with the GloboCorp company with an associate degree. I was working full time and going to school full time to continue my education. After I had graduated, I felt a sense of accomplishment but other than the piece of paper I got, it didn't really amount to much. My background was in engineering. The interesting part about the school that I went to was that none of my teachers had master's degrees. None. But they all had 20+ years of real-world industry experience.

The best bit of advice that they gave me was that If I wanted a job where I could start at the top, I should get a job digging ditches.

They explained to me that there were two ways to walk in the door. The first way was to start at an entry level. Learn the company, learn the people, learn the processes, and work my way up to being a proficient engineer. This was obviously a tough pill to swallow staring down student loan payments.

The second way was to go in right at the engineer level. You won't know the product or process; you won't know the company. As a direct result you won't get any respect from the people you work with, and most people who follow this path typically end up unemployed or in a lesser role withing 3 to 5 years.

All the while blaming everyone else for their failure because they weren't supported enough.

Not everyone will fall prey to the second way, just as not all who follow the first way are guaranteed to reach the level of success they desire. You may take the first path and realize the destination you were seeking wasn't all that it was cracked up to be. You may even find a different path along the way that you enjoy more. However, one thing is certain. Those who follow the first way have a better chance of staying with the organization longer, unlike those who decided to go in at the top level.

When thinking about this, I'm reminded of an interview I saw of Simon Sinek regarding new hires entering the workplace. He states that they want to make an impact on arrival. He told us to picture a large mountain. Paraphrasing his quote "The impact these new hires are looking to make is reaching the summit. It doesn't matter if you climb the mountain slowly, or quickly, but there's still a mountain you have to climb."

This is very accurate, degree or not.

Now, the other side of that group are the ones who have the BS, MS, and PHD's, and you would never know it. These people are highly intelligent, articulate and most importantly, grounded. They know what they don't know. These people are the shining example of what a college degree can do for a person where the previous group is a glaring indictment of the whole system.

These people will actively seek your counsel and look to learn the best practices and see how they can marry what they have learned in school with the practical applications of the organization. They are typically active listeners and people of few words. When they do speak though, people listen.

THAT is what you need to be on the lookout for. When you see people who command that kind of respect from those around you, you need to act like a sponge and absorb all that you can from that individual.

Now, in regard to those who don't have an advanced degree, don't think that I forgot about you.

People who are proud graduates from the school of hard knocks have a distinct advantage in that they are great at thinking on their feet and are quick at decision making. They have the benefit of past trial and error at their disposal and tend to operate independently with minimal support needed.

Now, just because you are quick to make a decision or quick to take action doesn't mean that it's the right action to take. Conventional wisdom typically serves these people well because they have seen how this movie ends before, and they know what pitfalls to avoid.

The problem with this kind of thinking is that you often get caught up in the trap of tradition and routine. I have stated earlier in the book that the most expensive words in the English language are "We've always done it this way". Well, that saying is this person's bible. That combined with "If it ain't broke, don't fix it" are the hallmark statements you can expect to hear.

When a new face shows up with new ideas, even if these ideas come from a classroom environment, they should not be so easily dismissed. But unfortunately, they will be. Be the person to take the time to listen to what people have to say. In today's society everyone is so wrapped up in social media echo chambers and virtue signaling that we only listen to respond. Very rarely do people listen to actually understand. You will be surprised at what people have to offer when you let them have a seat at the table with an open-mind policy, not just an open-door policy.

One thing that graduate degree employees have that others don't is a solid understanding of proven business theories and fundamentals, and also examples they learned in class from reviewing the best practices from other organizations. Even though it is only theory, it can be augmented and adapted to meet your organization's needs. This is how things like Six Sigma and ISO 9000 standards were created. Do they work in every application, no. For example, Six Sigma is terrible at adapting to variables. However, if you have a repetitive process that is the exact same every time, you can use someone who went to school for it to help be more efficient.

I always stated that Six Sigma was the equivalent of driving down the freeway doing 90 mph and only looking at the rear-view mirror. You adjusted your course based on the wake of debris and destruction you left behind. My industry had a lot of variables. So, when someone went out of their way to tell you they were a Six Sigma black belt, or green belt, or a Kaizen Facilitator, any input they provided was immediately in one ear, and out the other. Right, wrong, or indifferent, that is what happened. I know because I was a Kaizen Facilitator. I'm not proud of it.

When I applied that same knowledge to a manufacturing environment, everyone was all ears. You need to know your audience.

The problem with graduates from the school of hard knocks is that their teacher is scar tissue. They have a painful reminder that they received a great education of what *not* to do. The only problem with using this as a tool is that it's only beneficial to you when you encounter an issue or a problem that you have experienced before. If you try to apply it to a new issue, or new problem that arises, if anyone tells you the outcome was anything more than pure dumb luck, they are selling something. They got lucky. That's the thing with using trial and error, you have a 50/50 shot every time. Your solution is either going to work, or it isnt. Also, just because it worked doesn't mean that it didn't happen simply by accident. It also doesn't mean that your failure wasn't by accident either. The point is that until you come to that bridge, conventional wisdom can serve as a guide, but nothing more.

That is the point of this chapter. You need to do some self-scouting and self-realization to determine which path you find yourself on. Whichever path you discover is yours. Find people in your organization that complement your skillsets, and vice versa. This way whether you lean on knowledge or whether your lean on wisdom as a strength, when you work with someone who is on a different path, you both leave the exchange with more than what you came into it with. The best way to be able to obtain success in corporate America is to swallow your ego, and accept the fact that you don't know everything, regardless of if you have a degree or not. Try to view every conversation you have with someone as an opportunity to learn something new. Even if that something is to avoid future conversations with that person.

This is called humility.

Chapter Twelve

"No matter what door you choose to walk through, you can always get back to the hallway."

When I was younger, to say I was conflicted about what I wanted to do with my life would have been an understatement. My grandfather thought I should have become a lawyer or gotten into politics. My Aunt wanted me to be a priest, my mother wanted me to go to college, I wanted to join the military, and my father just wanted me to be better. Like most young people in their late teens, the world was still a mystery. I was shrouded in a deep fog of uncertainty, and no one was able to provide any kind of relatable insight that made sense. That was until I received another important message from my grandfather on the topic.

Walk with me down memory lane for a moment, won't you? I'm a conflicted 18-year-old trying to find out what I want to do with my life. I find myself in my grandfather's house. It was a small brick one and a half story house built in 1953. It wasn't elaborate or anything fancy. It was large enough to raise a family of 6, but small enough to know a working family lived there. My grandfather was always fond of saying "Be it ever so humble, there's no place like home". My grandfather sat me down on the couch in the living room, or as he liked to call it, "the parlor". He sat in a white recliner chair immediately to my right, and he looked at me and could tell I was conflicted with everything that was going on. I told you what everyone had expected of me. At that point in time, I had my heart set on joining the military and was hell-bent to make it happen as soon as I turned eighteen. As a World War II Air Force veteran, I would have assumed that my grandfather would have been sympathetic to my cause and given me clear direction on how to proceed that would have been in line with my intentions. Unfortunately, he was conflicted at the same time. You see he was caught between a rock and a hard place because my mother wanted me to go to college. What made it even more complicated was that my grandmother, (his wife, and my mom's mother) passed away on my 18th birthday. We were together for a birthday celebration where we were discussing what wonders life had yet to give as I was now becoming an adult, only to discover the harsh reality of what it can take away only 3 hours later. It was an unexpected heart attack that shook our entire family to the core.

I remember sitting with my grandfather after the wake in the room as I had described. What can you even say in a situation like that where someone passes so unexpectedly? Most people try to talk about anything else to keep their mind off of it.

My grandfather, though mourning, still maintained his composure and was able to provide insight to me as he always did.

He knew that my mother
was not fond of the
military. She had lost too
many friends to the
Vietnam war and didn't
want me to share a similar
fate. Now, combined with
the loss of my
grandmother, it only
compounded the gravity of
the situation. She had just
lost her mom; she didn't
want to lose me too. Which
was understandable.

He knew better than to
choose a side between his
grandson and his daughter.
It was a no-win scenario.
What he did instead was
dip into his wealth of
knowledge and wisdom and
took the opportunity to
give me some very
powerful insight.

We were discussing life and
all of the twists and turns
that it takes. Including the
sudden and unexpected
passing of loved ones.

He told me that life is
nothing but a long hallway.
He said to picture a very
long hallway with
thousands of rooms lining
both sides of the corridor.

Each door was a decision
that I had to make.
Whether it was to take a
new job, start a new
relationship, move to a new
city, join the military, go to
college, etc. He wanted to
make sure I knew that life
didn't discriminate between
work and personal life, so I
couldn't either. And
sometimes the only doors I
had to choose from were
bad options. And when you
only have bad options to
choose from, you choose
the lesser of two evils.

What he told me next was
something that was so
simple, yet I found it to be
incredibly profound at the
same time.

He told me *"No matter
which door you choose to
walk through, you can
always get back to the
hallway."*

Which seems so simple
right? If you don't like
something, why stay? If
you really want to go for
something, just do it. right?
That's what Nike says.

If it were only so simple.

The reality of it is this. As we have discussed earlier in the book, it IS that *simple*, it's just not that *easy*.

People have bills to pay, mouths to feed, reputations to uphold, people's lives are depending on them. They can't just uproot and move without a whole other set of circumstances coming into play. Some with dire consequences.

You see, what I have found is that in corporate America, the larger public organizations don't want you to know about the hallway. They want you to think that you are trapped, for obvious reasons. It's much cheaper to retain people than it is to go and recruit and retrain new employees. They will tell you things like, its no better anywhere else. They will boast about their benefits and rewards programs that other outfits won't be able to provide. They will cherry pick statistical evidence to prove they are a leader in the industry, and gaslight the employees that the ruthless hours and working conditions they are forced to endure are for their benefit.

I wish I could say that these companies have been unsuccessful in their efforts. Sadly, that isnt the case at all. In fact, I would say it's the exact opposite.

It's been my experience that most employees in corporate America don't see themselves as an empowered individual with a hallway full of choices. When they look at their situation, they view themselves more as a passenger on a freight train, where the freight train is the company, and working for them makes them the passenger. Every year that they spend with this company that train slowly picks up speed.

Just like riding in a train, you don't notice how fast you are going until you look out the side window. Most people are so overwhelmed with their daily tasks they find themselves shouting curse words at the clock when quitting time comes around. They have so much work left to do, and not enough time to do it, so they become blind to all else that moves.

They rarely get to "look out the window". The first time they get the opportunity to notice how fast the train is moving is usually around work anniversaries. They might get something like added vested benefits or added vacation for years of service.

That train continues to pick up speed when their years of service hits the next 401K contribution threshold. This is where the amount of money goes up that the organization matches for the employee's retirement. This used to be the case with pensions as well, but outside of public entities and trade unions, pensions are a thing of the past.

They see the train picking up speed again when they get merit raises and promotions. It gets even faster after every birthday

as you get closer and closer
to retirement and further
and further away from your
start date.

It gets to the point that this
train is moving so fast, that
when the passenger does
get a chance to look out the
side window, it's moving so
rapidly it would feel like it
would be imminent death if
you were to jump off.
That's where they get you.
They are banking on that
fear.

This only gets compounded
because not only are you
contemplating professional
suicide by jumping off a
speeding train, but you also
think you are going to leave
all of your fellow
passengers and friends you
made along the way. You're
left behind alone as the
train continues on without
you because you decided to
jump.

I know I felt that way. I'm
sure I'm not alone either.

I stayed at the GloboCorp
company probably about 4
years too long based on an

over-developed sense of loyalty.

Make no mistake, there is no loyalty in corporate America. You will find it in some smaller private organizations, but that loyalty usually comes with the caveat of lower pay and decreased benefits.

I'll try my best to summarize that feeling, but chances are if you have been in a similar situation, you know that there are few words that can do it justice. One that comes to mind for me is simply...despair.

It got to the point for me that the train car that I was in at that GloboCorp company was essentially on fire, and my career was going to be facing impending doom either way, so I decided to make that jump.

As I leapt from that freight train car, It felt as though it was in the middle of a cold, damp, dark night in a driving rainstorm. The kind of darkness you see in the dead of winter when you can't tell if it's the morning or nighttime. The train was moving so fast the raindrops felt like needles on my face. The wind generated by the train made each one feel like a miniature gunshot. Every time one hit me; It was a stinging memory of all the good times I had with this company. All the awards I had received, all the promotions, all the company parties, and picnics, happy hour, and golf leagues. All the hardship memories that brought me closer to my friends at work. All my mentors that had retired or passed away. All my hopes and dreams of what I thought this company could be was just engulfing me and piercing me like a swarm of angry hornets. I was suffocating from the pressure. As I turn midair to see the train speeding off into the distance and gravity pulling me toward the unknown, I can't help but think to myself,

"What am I doing?"

"Why did I jump?"

"Am I stupid for leaving?"

As the lights from the train fade into the distance, darkness begins to surround me again and the long cold reality of what I had decided to do begins to hit home.

Now, every one of those thoughts was one hundred percent valid. To be honest, I think I would have been more concerned if I had made a decision like that without contemplating all of the entangling consequences that awaited me.

Much like everyone else in corporate America, I believed that I was on that train for a good reason. And just like everyone else in corporate America who is still on that train, I was incredibly surprised on where I landed.

It wasn't some gloomy pit of despair, or nest of vipers, or booby-trapped abyss the likes that Indiana Jones often finds himself in. No, it wasn't that at all.

Much to my surprise, and also to some aspect, my shame, I landed in the hallway. Just like my grandfather said I would. That door closed. That door that I had spent 15 years behind had run its course and closed that chapter in my life. It was almost as if I had awakened from a bad dream. There was a sense of cathartic freedom. It was invigorating. The unknown potential was just as much intoxicating as it was terrifying.

I knew that my time on the train was going to be coming to an end sooner or later, and that I had to have some kind of a backup plan. After all, just like everyone else, I had a mortgage, a family, and responsibilities that have no sympathy and do not care if I am employed or not. So, I had put my resume out to several organizations prior to my jumping.

Much to my surprise because I had followed the methods I described in this book and tried to operate

with a high level of
character and integrity, the
reputation I had established
for myself preceded me. I
found myself with not just 1
but multiple job offers,
both in and outside of my
industry.

People wanted to work
with me. If for no other
reason than I was
passionate about what I
did, and they had seen me
deliver on what I said I
would do in the past.

I was honored and humbled
almost to the point of tears.
It had turned out that
everyone who had any kind
of interaction with that
GloboCorp company knew
the extents of how toxic it
was to work there. They
knew that the level of
quality of people that were
passionate, dedicated, and
willing to endure that place
day in and day out were
worth their salt. Not only
that, they also were worthy
of taking a chance on. This
is because there is one
truth in any organization,
not just corporate America.
You can teach people pretty

much anything you want
them to know.

However, you can't teach
"give a shit". That is
something that is either
engrained in you, or it isn't.
It's not something you can
fake. You can't go to school
for it. People can tell
immediately if you have it
or not. Some people may
refer to it as being genuine,
or authentic. The way
people can tell is because
it's not anything you say.
It's demonstrated in your
actions and how you carry
yourself.

The entire time I was at
that company all I was
trying to do was a good
enough job to get noticed
and gain recognition for my
hard work and dedication.
Little did I know that it *was*
noticed and recognized, just
not by whom I thought.
You have more contacts out
there than you may realize.

As soon as the word got out
on the street that I was
essentially a free agent, I
had gotten phone calls
from vendors and suppliers
I had worked with that I

didn't even apply to that were offering me positions to join them.

The hallway was real. I couldn't believe it. I wouldn't believe it. I had to see it with my own eyes before I would even acknowledge it existed.

Granted it would have been much easier if I would have just taken my grandfather's word for it way back when and used that advice to save me a bunch of heartache. But at the same time, I don't think I would have appreciated what he shared with me as much as I do today.

Now this doesn't mean that the hallway is always a good thing either. Like most things, it's a useful tool to know it's there, but just like any tool that isnt used properly it can be a source of danger as well.

Let me give you an example, let's say that you find yourself back in the hallway more often than you would like. Let's say that you are having a hard time identifying what you want to do for a career, or you are frequently changing companies or organizations in your industry.

When you are putting together your resume, recruiters and hiring managers will see these frequent flyer miles in the hallway and will view you as a migrant. A transient who is only "passing through" waiting for the next best opportunity. Essentially just a vagabond jumping from train to train.

They will be hesitant to take a chance on you because they don't believe you will be staying with them for any extended period of time beyond 2-3 years. The amount of money it takes to train and onboard you into their organization becomes cost prohibitive to take a chance.

This is why character building is so important. Putting up with adversity at times can be a good thing for the long run. In speaking with hiring managers one of the key thresholds when reviewing resumes was looking for people who stayed at one place for at least 5 years or longer. Often times they paid headhunters to try and steal away people who were already employed.

New hires coming into the workforce should be very excited to hear this. Most managers that I have spoken to would rather take a chance on some new blood coming into the workforce to give them a chance to prove themselves, than a high-priced free agent who has experience but doesn't typically stay around for more than 2 years. More importantly, that high priced free agent is on the street for a reason. One that most employers have no interest in finding out.

So, in essence, having no experience at times can also serve as an asset provided you have the right mindset and expectations when that opportunity presents itself. Because just like the main hallway, every door you enter that leads you to a new company, has a whole new hallway of doors within that company. Don't just look at the company for the door being presented to you today. Ask questions once you get there about what other doors are available to you 5 years from now, 10 years from now, etc. That kind of approach is more appealing to hiring managers because it shows you are willing to commit to a career with them. If you go in immediately looking for the door that leads to the corner office, you may find yourself back in the hallway sooner than you'd like.

So, the important thing to remember is that there is a hallway, it's safe to jump from the train and visit there. You may be surprised what you find when you get there, both good and bad. Just like any good vacation or tourist destination, it's a nice place to visit, but you definitely don't want to live or spend a considerable amount of time there.

There is no shame in having to go back to the hallway either. Sometimes you end up there because of circumstances beyond your control. Things like reduction in force, or layoffs happen. Just know that success isnt permanent, and failure isn't fatal. You just need to be willing to walk through that next door. Know that you have all of the tools necessary to succeed already in your arsenal. Your willpower is more powerful than you may think.

This is called self-reliance.

Chapter Thirteen

"You know you are living a good life, when your head hits your pillow, and you go right to sleep."

It's fitting that this is the last chapter of the book because this was the last bit of advice my grandfather ever gave me. There were more sayings that aren't included in this book, but this one was the last. My grandfather used to often say that *"you know you are living a good life when you your head hits your pillow, and you go right to sleep."*

When my grandfather told me this, I was still just a teenager. I remembered thinking to myself "Why wouldn't someone be able to sleep when they go to bed?" I didn't have any bills or any real responsibilities yet. It was a fun reminder about how naïve we are when we are younger. That and how we have so much we have yet to learn.

Now having grown up and experienced what life could throw at you, If I had a month, I couldn't name all the things on that list to keep you up at night.

I never really had any issues going to sleep as I was rising through the ranks at

GloboCorp. I was part of the rank and file. My hands were dirty, but my conscience was clean. I had made my way to my coveted engineering position and worked there for a few years. I had worked so hard to get to this point in my career finally reaching what, for so long, I considered to be the summit of my personal Mount Everest to climb. When I got to the top of that mountain, after a couple of years, I looked around and realized that the view from that mountain was closer to that of a bunny hill at a low budget ski resort in New Jersey than Everest. I wasn't being challenged anymore. My earning potential had plateaued, and I felt like I could offer more to help people.

The higher ups at GloboCorp in my area had a track record of making terrible decisions when hiring division managers. That 3–5-year carousel had come full circle, and there was a vacancy that opened up. I was high spirited, and motivated. So, I decided to put my hat in the ring for consideration for the job. I knew that whatever manager the higher ups decided on would be a jerk.

I brought up my intentions to apply to my coworkers in my office and asked them for their thoughts. As I expected, they all told me I was crazy. We all laughed about it for a bit, and then jokingly agreed on the whole situation. At least this way, my co-workers and I knew what kind of "jerk" we could expect. It was better to move forward with the "devil we know" versus the "devil we don't know."

I applied for the position, and after several panel interviews and some stiff competition from outside candidates, I was ultimately awarded the position. The tactics I had employed by volunteering to assist served to my benefit.

When I got settled into the position, I was now exposed to high level financials, and all of the responsibilities that came with operating a sixteen-million-dollar profit and loss statement. I understood the business and what needed to be done from an operational standpoint, but the education that I would learn over the next 4 years would dwarf anything I learned over the last 11.

In those first 11 years I learned the industry, software, policies, procedures, and technology. In these next 4 years I would need to learn how to manage people and politics.

Now mind you, this isn't just managing people who report to you, this is also learning how to manage the people that you report to as well, and how they interact with you and vice versa.

Seeing how the company generated and reported revenue, in contrast to the billing procedures, was a daily occurrence. Where the rubber met the road was when our key performance indicators

(KPI) on our employee's performance were down and revenue and billing was impacted.

Difficult decisions needed to be made at times. That was part of the role and I understood that. There were times when employees were just not up to the company standard. These instances happened for various reasons. After they were given every opportunity to turn it around, the time ultimately came where they needed to find happiness elsewhere.

I used to sarcastically joke and lash out in frustration when cleaning up someone else's mess that this person who made the mess should be fired for all the trouble they caused. That was until the day came when I actually had to let somebody go. The one thing I learned here is that people who joke around about firing someone, have never actually done it. I don't joke around about it anymore. I would also go as far as to say that anyone in a management role who does joke around about it should seriously re-evaluate their priorities.

I remember one instance where I had interviewed a candidate for a leadership position. I asked them "What is your dream job?". Their answer shocked me. It still does to this day. Their answer to the question was:

"I just want a job where I can fire people".

Now, this candidate was very young and fresh out of school. I am not one to pile on the millennial generation, but this person did not represent them well.

I gave him an opportunity to clarify his statement, and when I dug a little deeper, his intention was that he wanted to have "a management role where he had influence over the team he worked with." I told him in the future you may not want to use that initial response again.

Even when I had the odious task of delivering someone the news their employment was terminated, I still had a clean conscience because I knew I gave that person every opportunity to right the ship. They chose not to take advantage of those opportunities. I had to view it as they ultimately fired themselves. These employees knew it as well, and I rarely had any outbursts or drama when delivering the bad news. That was being a good manager in my opinion.

Now when you get to the messy side of this topic with corporate America, the story changes. Every company has their own terms for it. Whether it be a Reduction-In-Force (RIF), layoffs, down-sizing, or the even more pretentious term "Right-sizing" the result is the same. Your headcount is going down, and not for the right reasons.

We were often given an excel spreadsheet to complete called a "Stack-

Ranking" where you essentially had to put all of your employees up on an auction block. The lowest value employees were almost always cut. The stack ranking form was given the dubious nickname of the "Rank and Yank".

The word came down from Corporate HQ, usually during the slowest quarter of the fiscal year that headcount needed to be trimmed by 10% across the board. The worst part about it is that we weren't losing money. We were actually highly profitable. We just weren't highly profitable enough.

I can remember the first time I had a completely sleepless night. It was right after the instructions came down that a RIF needed to take place, and what was worse is that I didn't get any input on which employees were being cut. It was pre-determined based on position.

Robert Jones was a happy go lucky person who by all accounts could be considered Mr. Sunshine. He always had a positive attitude. He always worked hard in role. The customers and employees loved him. He was known for having a tremendous sense of humor and playing practical jokes to help raise morale. He knew which buttons he could push, and when to get the biggest laughs. He was also my best friend.

Robert was on vacation when the RIF orders came down from Corporate, and his name was on the list. The command was issued late on a Thursday afternoon to all managers that the RIF was to be carried out the next morning on Friday. I had caught a lot of flack and grief from my superiors because I refused to fire a man when he was on vacation. I wasn't going to call a man up while he is with his family and fire someone over the phone. But that is what they wanted.

I refused. That was the starting point where my

superiors started to view me in a different light.

The following Monday came, and I was commanded to meet with Robert immediately. He didn't even get the chance to take his coat off, or even get a sip of his morning coffee.

To his credit, Robert was the ultimate professional. I explained to him the situation, and he understood completely. Robert remained true to form and was even able to joke about it.

He told me, "I get it. It's business. Don't be upset about it. You're Paul Revere, you aren't the British."

What happened next was inexplicably the worst sequence of events I could have ever imagined. I wish that I was making this up, but it really happened.

Corporate in their infinite wisdom decided to enforce the call of letting Robert go on Monday, April 1st. That's right. April Fool's Day.

Robert, a renown practical jokester after completing his exit paperwork began making phone calls to his fellow co-workers that he had been with for over a decade to say his final goodbyes and well wishes. One by one, over and over again. Robert would call them up and tell them he was let go and it was nice working with them. Almost every single person he worked with responded in kind with "Very funny Bob, April Fools!" and then hung up. Not only was he fired by his best friend the day he came back from vacation, after doing a good job, for no good reason, but he also couldn't even get the chance to say goodbye. We were a field service organization, so he had a company fleet vehicle assigned to him. I was responsible for driving him home. I broke down into tears halfway through. The whole situation was heart wrenching.

The outrage from the rest of the team in the following days when they found out it wasn't an April's fools day joke was tangible. To this day, few have ever gotten over the disservice done to that man.

Having to fire my best friend in that manner, and having to answer to his family, his friends, both in and outside of work remains one of the worst days in my career. One that I often use as a measuring stick for comparison.

I didn't sleep one wink that night.

When things started to really go askew for me at GloboCorp was when I got to see how they wanted to handle their financial reporting. They were a public company and regulated by the SEC so there were many hoops and barrels you needed to jump through and over to make sure you stayed out of hot water with Wall Street.

Every year you would hear a collective groan from every employee in the company when they would roll out roughly 8 hours of online compliance and ethics, and regulatory training on the company's policies. They stressed how if you saw something unethical it was your duty to report, and that failure to report it would result in disciplinary action. For some people it could even potentially result in jail time.

I had noticed a trend that was occurring not only with my location's numbers, but numbers across the entire company. They weren't adding up, numbers were being manipulated to artIfIcially inflate my bosses' yearend bonuses. All to the detriment of the employees, the customers, and the company as a whole. When I raised these concerns at the local level, to say that they were abruptly dismissed would be an understatement.

Keeping in line with what I thought was doing the right thing, I raised awareness up the food chain that money had been manipulated to the tune of roughly two hundred and fifty thousand dollars. The local management was essentially cooking the books. When I dug into it further, I was floored to find out that it had been going on for the better part of seven years.

I knew it wasn't right. I valued my integrity, so I did the right thing, or so I thought, and called it in to my superiors.

What did I get for my efforts in recognition in doing the "right thing"?

Corporate went out of their way to fly in a representative from oversees to personally invite me to a forensic audit. For those who are unfamiliar with what a forensic audit is, it's where they will go through every single line in your P&L statement, all the way down to the individual line item of every purchase order you have ever issued, every bill you ever generated, and every red cent you ever collected. Its is excruciatingly painful.

Within a week, they had confirmed the person responsible for cooking the books and let him go to satisfy corporate. Just as point of clarification. This person was not a bad man. I personally believe he simply succumbed to the pressure of the role he was in trying to meet an unrealistic target. It compromised his judgement, and ultimately his integrity along with it. I think he made poor choices, but I never held it against him personally, my reporting his behavior was a business decision only. You couldn't pay me enough to want his job.

Much to my surprise the superior that I raised awareness to is the one that came in to terminate him. After the superior finished with the termination, he came into my office and thanked me for identifying the irregularities in the numbers. What he said next would shock me to the core.

He told me that even though he knew that the numbers were false, and that we knew what needed to be done to right the wrong and correct things. His instructions to me were:

"You need to fix this within five months because that is fiscal year end, and this better not be an exercise in math."

My heart fell into my stomach. I had known this person for over 15 years, he hired me, and mentored me. I always held him in the highest regard as a pillar of integrity. It wasn't just me. Everyone loved him. It was the reason I raised awareness to him in the first place. To now be presented with this statement was soul crushing.

He didn't *want* it fixed.

He knew that fixing it would negatively affect his bonus as well and the region as a whole. That was something he wasn't willing to accept.

What's worse is that he knew it took seven years to

get this bad, and he didn't care. He gave me five months to overcome a loss of two hundred and fifty thousand dollars in profits knowing full well it was a physical impossibility to accomplish in the time permitted with the backlog that we had available. All the while knowing, I was going to be facing an impending forensic audit that would cannibalize my time.

He wasn't just setting me up to fail. He was signing off on my professional death sentence at the company.

He was looking to make an example of someone who didn't want to play ball. This was like something right out of HBO's Game of Thrones. I was beside myself.

I soon found out the reason why.

Because the dollar value was so outlandish it would appear that one head was not enough. The company needed a head on a stake to set an example and to show Wall Street. My superior was going to be damn certain that head wouldn't be his. But I wasn't going to go quietly into the night either. You remember earlier in the book when I referred to my train car being on fire right before I jumped. Well, you were just introduced to the arson.

Because I followed the tactics listed in this book, my documentation was meticulous and accurate. For that reason, this forensic audit ended up lasting for the better part of five months. It lasted that long because there was nothing to find. I knew what the end objective was, and it wasn't going to end well for me. Eventually they would find an honest mistake, and that is what they would hang their hat on right before they would strike. I wasn't willing to let that happen. True to form with these management positions in corporate America that typically last 3 -5 years. My tenure ended

at 4. That piece of wood
that I was given when I took
this position ended up
being a plank that I would
walk out the door on. But I
vowed to myself it would
be on my terms. Not theirs.

Over those last five months,
if I averaged an hour of
sleep a night, that was a
good night. I got out of bed
every single morning with
the expectation that.
"Today's the day". Todays
the day that they find that
honest mistake and fire me.
I repeated that morning
mantra to prepare myself
for the inevitable every
morning for five months. I
was working 80-hour
weeks. I had to conduct the
forensic audit from 7:00am
to 3:30pm every day, and
then once the audit was
done for the day, I still had
my regular job that I had to
perform, and failure wasn't
an option.

Despite being set up for
failure, I was efficient
enough that I was still able
to find some degree of
success. But it came with a
very heavy toll. I was a

wreck. My blood pressure was through the roof, I had no family or personal life, and barely ever saw daylight outside of working hours.

Despite all of my adversity I was still trying to make it work. I had looked at my numbers in comparison to other regions to get a barometer on where I was going to end up. What I had noticed was that all of the other regions in GloboCorp were making the most absurd of decisions. They were cutting high-cost revenue generating positions, and letting maintenance of existing equipment slip, all the while whipping the sales team for more production. This wasn't a short-term trend either. I had noticed this happening consistently over my five months under the microscope. I thought to myself, statistically speaking, they should have *accidentally* made a good decision by now, but they didn't. Someone was intentionally driving the company into the ground at full speed ahead. They were making the company show record profits, all while slitting their financial throat in the process. It was only a matter of time that they would ask me to do the same thing at my location.

I was done. I had enough. I had been recruited by several other organizations over the years and had respectfully declined their offers. I had resumes out on the street but was also contacted by some of these companies again that I didn't apply to. I decided the tIme was right to finally jump from this flaming train car. I was mentally and physically exhausted and on the brink of requiring medication to get my blood pressure under control.

So, I made the jump. It would appear that I also did it just in the nick of time.

Within 6 months of me leaving GloboCorp, they closed 21 offices, and fired every general manager in all 140 locations. Then they sold the company.

GloboCorp was no more.
Good riddance.

In my new role, I was able
to use the tactics that I
have described in this book.
I became familiar with a
previously foreign concept
called "work/life balance".
I was able to see my wife,
my friends, and my family
again. Much to my surprise
I was even able to keep in
close contact with many of
my former colleagues that I
had at GloboCorp.

I didn't change my diet. I
didn't change my exercise
habits, I didn't change a
thing except my work
environment, and within 6
months, my blood pressure
was normal.

I have since gone on to help
build two successful
businesses from scratch
using these methods and
tactics and have never slept
better. Now, when my head
hits the pillow, I fall right to
sleep. I think my
grandfather would consider
this as living a good life.

This is called having inner peace.

The End.

A Note from the Author

I would once again like to truly thank you for taking the time to read this book. It is deeply appreciated.

If the failures, trials, and tribulations I experienced help provide some value to you on your journey down your career path, this book is already a tremendous success.

If you have found it helpful and know of others who you believe could benefit from it, please share it with them.

You can also share your feedback with me on X (Formerly Twitter) @_Daniel_Vaccaro

With Sincere Thanks,

Daniel Vaccaro